3D Reconstruction with Deep Learning

Rocher

Copyright © [2023]

Author: Rocher

Title: . 3D Reconstruction with Deep Learning

This book is a self-published work by the author Rocher

ISBN:

Abstract

One of the major challenges in the field of Computer Vision has been the reconstruction of a 3D object or scene from a single 2D image. While there are many notable examples, traditional methods for single view reconstruction often fail to generalise due to the presence of many brittle hand-crafted engineering solutions, limiting their applicability to real world problems. Recently, deep learning has taken over the field of Computer Vision and "learning to reconstruct" has become the dominant technique for addressing the limitations of traditional methods when performing single view 3D reconstruction. Deep learning allows our reconstruction methods to learn generalisable image features and monocular cues that would otherwise be difficult to engineer through ad-hoc hand-crafted approaches. However, it can often be difficult to efficiently integrate the various 3D shape representations within the deep learning framework. In particular, 3D volumetric representations can be adapted to work with Convolutional Neural Networks, but they are computationally expensive and memory inefficient when using local convolutional layers. Also, the successful learning of generalisable feature representations for 3D reconstruction requires large amounts of diverse training data. In practice, this is challenging for 3D training data, as it entails a costly and time consuming manual data collection and annotation process. Researchers have attempted to address these issues by utilising self-supervised learning and generative modelling techniques, however these approaches often produce suboptimal results when compared with models trained on larger datasets. This thesis addresses several key challenges incurred when using deep learning for "learning to reconstruct" 3D shapes from single view images. We observe that it is possible to learn a compressed representation for multiple categories of the 3D ShapeNet dataset, improving the computational and memory efficiency when working with 3D volumetric representations. To address the challenge of data acquisition, we leverage deep generative models to "hallucinate" hidden or latent novel viewpoints for a given input image. Combining these images with depths estimated by a self-supervised depth estimator and the known camera properties, allowed us to reconstruct textured 3D point clouds without any ground truth 3D training data. Furthermore, we show that is is possible to improve upon the previous self-supervised monocular depth estimator by adding a self-attention and a discrete volumetric representation, significantly improving accuracy on the KITTI 2015 dataset and enabling the estimation of uncertainty depth predictions.

List of Tables

List of Figures

CHAPTER 1

Introduction

1.1 Motivations

Developing artificial systems that emulate or rival some of the capabilities of the human visual system has long been a goal of Computer Vision researchers. Computer Vision contains many sub-disciplines concerned with solving a variety of visual problems. For instance, the task of recovering the three-dimensional (3D) world using images or video is known as 3D reconstruction. As with many problems in Computer Vision, 3D reconstruction is considered an *inverse problem* [323], where researchers attempt to recover some information about the world (e.g., 3D shape of visual objects and their relative pose) given insufficient and ambiguous visual data. As a result, we must often rely heavily on physical [135, 272, 358], mathematical [121, 331] and probabilistic models [52, 277, 363] to create 3D reconstructions.

3D reconstruction of scenes and objects is of general scientific interest and forms part of core technologies used in a wide range of problems. More specifically, it has applications in Computer Graphics, Computer Vision, Medical Imaging, Virtual/Augmented Reality (VR/AR), Geology and many other scientific fields. Many robotic applications require the mapping of the 3D environment to avoid obstacles and to perform path planning. This technique is known as Simultaneous Localisation and Mapping or SLAM [314, 315] and is widely applied in autonomous vehicles [352], drones [313], and consumer robotics [179]. While the maps created by SLAM systems need not necessarily be full 3D reconstructions, in many applications, dense 3D reconstructions are preferred. For example, robotic vacuum cleaners do not require a full 3D map to successfully navigate an environment, but autonomous drones require 3D reconstruction as they operate in all three dimensions and must therefore plan their path in 3D to avoid obstacles. Moreover, many self-driving car systems utilise pre-made 3D maps reconstructed from the environment in which the car is expected to operate. Often these environments are scanned using a combination of range-finding sensors like LiDAR and passive cameras. These 3D reconstructions can then be utilised as part of a SLAM system for localising the autonomous vehicle within its environment. 3D reconstruction is not limited to robotic applications. For instance, the in-built camera and rich sensor data captured from modern smart phones have enabled the development of several commercially available games based on 3D reconstruction techniques, to create immersive and engaging augmented reality game-play experiences [68,353]. Furthermore, several commercially available VR/AR headsets use 3D reconstruction for mapping and localisation. These 3D reconstructions can be integrated with the VR experience to ensure that users do not collide with unseen obstacles, or in augmented reality headsets for projecting user interfaces [257]. 3D Reconstruction has also been used for preserving cultural sites in Archaeology [32], for urban planning [6] and for various applications in medical imaging [377,386].

In many applications, it may not be possible to deploy 3D reconstruction systems that utilise multiple cameras or active range-finding, due to cost, efficiency or design constraints. For example, small drones often cannot leverage active range finding or traditional stereo vision due to limited battery capacity or insufficient camera baselines. In these cases, it may be preferential to perform single view 3D reconstruction, where we are given a single image at run time to try and recover the underlying 3D object or scene. This is considered one of the most challenging problems in Computer Vision [323]. Methods for Single-View 3D reconstruction traditionally focused on exploiting monocular perception cues such as shading [135, 136], image focus/defocus [272], and texture [358]. However, using these monocular cues for single view reconstruction poses many challenges, as each of these techniques make assumptions regarding lighting, material and surface properties. In practice this often limits these methods to work exclusively within constrained environments.

Many classical 3D reconstruction methods use multiple views of a surface to recover the underlying geometry. Typically, these algorithms rely on hand-crafted local feature descriptors for matching image regions captured from different viewpoints. The feature correspondences can then be triangulated to reconstruct a depth map or 3D surface. However, these traditional feature extraction methods require image regions to have distinguishable (i.e., non-repeatable) texture, which, depending on application, can result in sub-optimal 3D reconstruction. As these feature extraction methods were initially developed to enable matching of image regions, they are designed to be robust to small changes in scale or orientation, while attempting to preserve their ability to distinguish between non-corresponding patches. This leads to a complicated trade-off between robustness and discriminative ability, which must be engineered for the task of interest. Furthermore, as these descriptors are hand-crafted, they are often time consuming to develop and fail to capture higher level semantic or contextual information, leading to sub-optimal generalisation in both 3D reconstruction and other Computer Vision tasks. To address the sub-optimality of local feature descriptors, researchers apply a class of techniques known as deep learning, to many problems in Computer Vision. Deep learning models are typically represented by Artificial Neural Networks [124, 236, 295], which are trained in an end-to-end fashion using gradient descent, to learn feature representations that can solve a task of interest. In many areas of Machine Learning and Computer Vision, "learning" feature representations has shown significant improvement over hand-designed feature descriptors [106]. Models trained in this manner are known as Deep Neural Networks (DNNs).

DNNs have shown outstanding progress in the reconstruction of 3D objects and scenes from monocular images [52, 98, 364]. However, single view 3D reconstruction remains one of the most challenging tasks in Computer Vision, as any method that aims to accurately recover the scene or object of interest must leverage a range of monocular cues. Historically, exploiting these cues in a generalisable manner has proven difficult. Deep learning offers one possible solution by allowing the reconstruction methods to indirectly "learn" the monocular cues and representations necessary for recovering the 3D surface of interest.

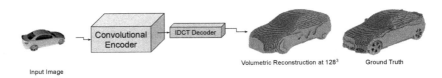

Input Image   Convolutional Encoder   IDCT Decoder   Volumetric Reconstruction at 128^3 Ground Truth

Figure 1.1: Overview of the volumetric reconstruction using an Inverse Discrete Cosine Transform layer to achieve highly efficient 3D reconstruction.

While its successes are numerous, applying deep learning to 3D reconstruction presents several challenges. Firstly, deep learning models require large amounts of computational resources to train effectively which can be further exacerbated by the choice of shape representations. For example, 3D volumes are often an order of magnitude larger than the equivalent 2D images, leading to significant inefficiencies when using these representations with deep learning models. This leads to a trade off between reconstruction quality, and computation and memory usage. Secondly, training accurate and generalisable Deep Neural Networks requires immense amounts of diverse cleanly labelled data, which is often unavailable for tasks such as 3D reconstruction. This issue of data scarcity limits the applicability of 3D deep learning based reconstruction systems in real world applications. Researchers have proposed a variety different model training regimes to address this, such as transfer learning [106], self-supervised learning and semi-supervised learning using generative models [106]. However, a third challenge is that these methods do not currently reach the same levels of quantitative performance as models trained with full supervision. Therefore, to enable the wider adoption of deep learning in real world systems, it is becoming increasingly important develop models that need significantly less labelled training data, but are also accurate as fully supervised methods.

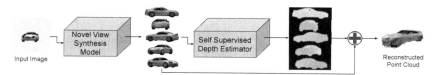

Figure 1.2: Overview of single image 3D point cloud reconstruction.

This thesis aims to develop techniques to address the challenges of computational efficiency and data scarcity when training deep neural networks for monocular 3D reconstruction and depth estimation. We describe several novel techniques for addressing the challenges of applying deep learning to the problem of single view 3D reconstruction. We present a method for single view 3D reconstruction which simultaneously improves reconstruction resolution, computational usage and memory consumption, by an order of magnitude when compared with the baseline method [52] – see Figure 1.1. We also propose a framework for single view point cloud reconstruction that utilises novel view prediction and self-supervised depth estimation to recover textured 3D point clouds with no ground truth 3D training data – see Figure 1.2. Finally, we show that by applying self-attention and a discrete volumetric representation, it is possible to significantly improve the accuracy of self-supervised depth estimation, compared with the current state of the art [103], and to enable the estimation of uncertainty from these depth predictions – see Figure 1.3.

1.2   Contributions

The main contributions of this thesis are as follows:

- We demonstrate how to efficiently perform single image 3D volumetric reconstruction at high resolutions using an end to end deep learning model with a novel Inverse Discrete Cosine Transforms (IDCT) Layer. We show how

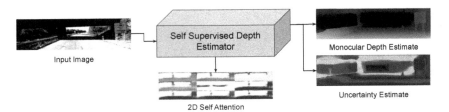

Figure 1.3: Overview of Self-Supervised Depth estimation.

the performance is improved by an order of magnitude in terms of memory consumption and computational efficiency, allowing for significantly higher resolution reconstructions (Figure 1.1).

• We present a framework for single image 3D point cloud reconstruction that does not require any 3D ground truth data for training, obviating the need for costly manual data acquisition. We show that by leveraging deep generative models and Self-Supervised Depth Estimators it is possible to reconstruct high quality textured point clouds using only sets of images for training (Figure 1.2).

• We also demonstrate how to improve the reconstruction accuracy and esti- mate reconstruction uncertainty of self-supervised monocular depth estima- tors by incorporating 2D self-attention and a discrete disparity volume. We show how the large receptive field afforded by the self-attention operation improves the modelling capabilities of the estimator. Furthermore, by con- straining the model to use a discrete volumetric representation of disparity, we are also able to estimate the depth estimate uncertainty (Figure 1.3).

1.3   Thesis Structure

The structure of the thesis is as follows. In Chapter 2 we review the prior art, its history and how it relates to 3D reconstruction using deep learning. Chapter 3 contains an overview of the methods and components used in the body chapters of this thesis. In Chapter 4 we show how using dimensionality reduction, in the form of the Inverse Discrete Cosine Transform (IDCT), can be integrated into a deep Convolutional Neural Network to drastically improve memory consumption and computational efficiency when working with sparse data such as 3D volumes (Figure 1.1). We show the improvements of our algorithm by performing Single View 3D Reconstruction on multiple categories of the ShapeNet [39] dataset and compare our method against the state of the art system of the time. In Chapter 5, we leverage the advances in deep generative modelling and self-supervised learning to perform single view 3D point cloud reconstruction. We first train a model to "hallucinate" novel view points of a given object using a Generative Adversarial Network [107], then we train a self-supervised depth estimator [94,101,103,339] to estimate partial 3D point clouds for each of the novel view points. This allowed us to reconstruct 3D textured point clouds without any 3D training data (Figure 1.2), alleviating the need for costly manual data collection. In Chapter 6, we focus on improving the Self-Supervised depth estimation techniques used in Chapter 5 by changing the internal representation of depth used by the model to a discrete disparity volume and by incorporating a self-attention mechanism allowing the network to model longer range relationships between pixels (Figure 1.3). Finally, Chapter 7 discusses the overall conclusions and suggested directions for future research.

CHAPTER 2

Literature Review

This chapter discusses the related background and relevant papers to clarify the context of this thesis. The first section covers a variety of techniques that have traditionally been used for 3D reconstruction. Concretely, it contains background information on methods for stereo matching in binocular imagery [323], monocular 3D reconstruction using Shape-from-X techniques [135, 272, 323, 358], the use of Active Range-finding sensors [323], simultaneous 3D reconstruction and pose estimation with Structure from Motion [331], and model-based reconstruction using 3D shape priors [323].

Many of the traditional 3D reconstruction algorithms rely on the use of hand-crafted feature descriptors [18, 61, 224] that were designed to allow the matching of a sparse set of image regions captured from different viewpoints. Given that these features are hand-designed, they cannot provide any optimality guarantee for the 3D reconstruction problem. This issue has always been the main motivation for the development of pure machine learning methods that not only learn how to reconstruct 3D scenes from 2D images, but also learn optimal image features for a given problem. Therefore, recent years have seen a resurgence of representation learning techniques based on Artificial Neural Networks (ANNs) [124, 236, 295] in an field known as deep learning [197]. The second section of this chapter covers representation learning with deep learning, discussing the fundamentals of Convolutional Neural Networks (CNNs) [90, 198] and deep generative models [106, 107, 176].

The final section discusses the applicability of incorporating traditional geometric Computer Vision techniques with the representational learning power of deep learning [106, 197]. Specifically, this section covers how shape priors can be learnt using deep learning for model-based reconstruction [52, 98, 364], how depth can be estimated from a single monocular image by casting it as a supervised learning problem [73, 74], and how self-supervised learning can be used to reduce the burden of capturing large amounts of depth and 3D training data [94, 101, 103, 339, 370].

2.1 3D Reconstruction

3D reconstruction is the process of recovering a 3D model of an object or a scene given one or multiple images that were captured using either a passive or active camera sensor (e.g LiDAR) [323]. Recovering 3D surfaces from images has always been a challenging goal and is considered one of the fundamental problems in Computer Vision [323]. Classically, binocular vision was used to obtain 3D information by using the triangulation of points between two synchronized cameras [119]. This triangulation often results in a depth measurement for each pixel, which is used to build a depth map or depth image. Recovering 3D surfaces from monocular images is considerably more difficult than from binocular images, as monocular 3D reconstruction relies on using one or more unsynchronized images captured from the same passive camera sensor. In practice, many different monocular cues can be used to extract three dimensional information from images [323], including texture, silhouettes, shading, focus and motion. Moreover, in cases where we know prior information about the surfaces to be reconstructed, we can rely on model-based reconstruction methods to simplify solving this inverse problem [323]. An alternative to the exclusive reliance on passive cameras is to use active range-finding sensors to facilitate the process of 3D reconstruction [256, 323].

This section discusses in detail the various traditional methods for 3D reconstruction using sets of binocular and monocular image(s). Furthermore, it covers the use of active range-finding sensors for capturing depth information, along with how this can be leveraged to create accurate 3D surfaces. Finally, we discuss how *a priori* information can be leveraged, in the form of shape priors, to improve reconstruction results.

2.1.1 Stereo Matching

In traditional stereo vision, two synchronized passive cameras are used to capture two different viewpoints of a scene. These two images are then used for estimating the depth image or 3D surfaces of a scene by finding and triangulating pixel correspondences between viewpoints [121, 323]. This technique is closely related to Stereopsis [138], which humans and many animals use to perceive the 3D world, through binocular disparity (i.e., the difference in appearance between our left and right eyes). In Computer Vision, the task of stereo matching has been one of the most widely researched topics and is considered one of the fundamental problems in the field [323]. While the basic physics and geometry of stereo vision is well understood [121], automatically measuring the disparity using pixel correspondences is a difficult task. In the simplest case, finding stereo correspondences requires a computationally expensive process which exhaustively searches for and matches local feature descriptors between the image pairs. Moreover, traditional feature descriptors require large areas of distinguishable textural detail to accurately find correspondences, while areas with heavily repeated texture (e.g. painted walls or carpeted floors) are often difficult to match correctly, resulting in sparse or inaccurate 3D reconstructions. Regardless, stereo vision has been heavily applied in many commercial systems due to its simplicity and cost effectiveness.

2.1.2 Multi View Stereo and Structure from Motion

While it is possible to match stereo correspondences to obtain accurate depth information, this is often insufficient for capturing full 3D shapes due to large occluded regions and limited stereo baseline, resulting in only partial 3D reconstruction. Multi-View Stereo (MVS) extends the idea of matching stereo correspondences, by solving the problem of reconstructing a 3D shape given an arbitrary number of images with known camera locations [121, 323]. Often, MVS setups are employed to capture full 3D surfaces for use in the entertainment industry, to create accurate 3D assets for VideoFX (VFX) and video games [306]. MVS relies on capturing synchronized images from multiple cameras at known camera locations. However, in practice, photographing multiple synchronized views needs careful calibration of multiple cameras that often require expensive hardware.

Structure from Motion (SfM) improves upon Multi-View Stereo by relaxing the constraint of requiring known synchronised view points [323]. Instead, SfM techniques jointly estimate the 3D geometry of a scene and the 3D motion of a camera given a sequence of images. To achieve this goal, features are first detected in each of the images in the sequence, and then these features are matched in other images and further refined using Random Sample Consensus (RANSAC) [85]. Then, nonlinear least squares is used to solve for the camera matrix for each image. Using the estimated camera matrix and feature correspondences, the same triangulation process that is employed in MVS can be applied to recover the 3D surface. SfM has been used to perform city scale reconstructions using large heterogeneous sets of images captured by the general public [7].

2.1.3   Shape-From-X

Binocular disparity is not the only visual cue used to perceive depth. It is thought that humans and animals utilise a range of different monocular cues in the absence of binocular vision to perceive the 3D world. While motion parallax [82], Depth from motion [146] and the relative size of objects are all strong cues for binocular vision, image shading [135,136], texture [358] and focus [272] have all been studied to reconstruct 3D surfaces from monocular images. The study of how these cues are used in Computer Vision is commonly referred to as *Shape-from-X* [323].

The task of recovering the 3D shape of a surface from variations in pixel intensities due to the illumination of the surface, is known as *shape from shading* [135] and is one of the earliest examples of single-view 3D reconstruction. By making assumptions about the material properties of the surface and the type of light source being applied, it is possible to invert the rendering equation and recover the surface normals and depth for each pixel in the image [323]. To recover the 3D model, most shape from shading algorithms make assumptions regarding the uniformity of the albedo and reflectance properties of the surface being reconstructed [323].

Furthermore, the direction of the illumination is assumed to be known *a priori* or can be calculated ahead of time [323]. In practice, these assumptions are extremely constraining and limit the use of *shape from shading* techniques in real world applications. Photometric stereo is one way to improve the reliability of *shape from shading*, where multiple light sources are selectively turned on and off creating multiple reflectance maps, which can be used to reconstruct surfaces with an unknown albedo [323]. However, this is still limited to environments, where the illumination can be carefully controlled.

Shape from texture relies on the fore-shorting of regular textural patterns to estimate information about a 3D surface [323]. The main processes used in *shape from texture* can be distilled into two main phases. First, the distortion of the texture is measured and then these measurements are used to recover the 3D coordinates of the surface [323]. While it is possible to extract some 3D information from textural details, many regions of real world images are texture-less or have low frequency detail, limiting the applicability of this technique.

An interesting observation that can be explored in *Shape-from-X* methods is that, as a surface moves away from the focal plane of the camera sensor, the associated pixels in the image will become more blurred (i.e., out of focus). *Shape from focus* is the method of extracting depth or a 3D surface by exploiting the blurring that occurs in images as the focal distance changes [80, 323]. One of the challenges of *shape from focus* is that the blurring increases in both directions moving away from the focal plane [80, 323]. Therefore, multiple images need to be captured at different focal lengths to accurately recover the surface. Furthermore, it is assumed that each image is capturing at extremely small exposure time to limit the amount of motion blur between shots.

2.1.4 Shape Representations

Up until now this review has not covered the exact representations that are used when working with 3D shapes. There are many ways to represent a 3D surface and they can mainly be categorised into three major groups; explicit Surfaces representations such as polygonal meshes and splines [323], point based representations in the form of point clouds [323] and volumetric representations such as binary voxel grids or signed distance fields [323]. Surface representations are one of the most readily available sources of 3D data due to their applications in Computer Graphics and Computer Aided Design. Polygonal meshes (Figure 2.1), which are one of the most common forms of surface representation, store 3D surfaces as a collection of vertices (3D points), faces and edges, where each face consists of triangles, quadrilaterals or other convex polygons to create a 3D graph [323]. These representations enable the creation of highly detailed models, as well as special operations, like interpolation, subdivision and non-rigid transformations (animation) [323]. However, one of the downsides of meshes is that the topology of the 3D graph must be fixed and known ahead of time and, therefore, this representation can be challenging to work when performing 3D reconstruction.

Figure 2.1: Rendering of a 3D car mesh from the ShapeNet [39] dataset. Left: Smooth shaded with ambient occlusion Right: Wireframe rendering showing the polygonal mesh structure.

Point clouds are represented as an un-ordered set of 3D coordinates where each point corresponds to a sample along a 3D surface [323] (Figure 2.2). Unlike surface meshes, we are only storing the 3D points and therefore do not need to know the topology of the graph [323]. Often, when working with large collections of 3D point clouds, it is essential to down-sample the set to a fixed number of points and then register correspondences between instances [323].

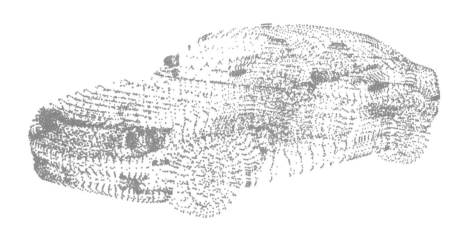

Figure 2.2: Rendering of a 3D car point cloud, from the ShapeNet [39] dataset.

3D volumes are an alternative way of representing 3D surfaces as a fixed size and uniform grid (Figure 2.3). These grids are either stored as a binary occupancy grid, where cell values represent voxel occupancy or as a signed distance field, where voxels represent distances to the zero level set that represents the surface boundary [323].

Figure 2.3: Rendering of a 3D car from the ShapeNet [39] dataset voxelized at 32^3 (left), 64^3 (middle) and 128^3 (right).

2.1.5   Active Rangefinding Sensors

While passive cameras offer one means of recovering 3D surfaces, reconstruction techniques often rely on the accurate detection and matching of feature descriptors from images. However, hand-crafted feature descriptors do not work well in areas of low frequency textural detail or of regions of repetitive texture, limiting the accuracy of correspondence-based reconstruction systems. Another possible approach to 3D reconstruction is to modify the camera hardware to actively sense the 3D world. Unlike stereo cameras, which have limited precision depending on the camera baseline, active sensors project light into the environment to measure 3D depth images. These active range-finding sensors are usually split into two categories. The first category is represented by structured light scanners, which recover 3D depth information by measuring the deformation of a known illumination pattern (uniform grid or horizontal bar) that is projected into the environment by the sensor [323]. It is often desirable to jointly recover RGB textural detail alongside 3D depth information. Therefore, the illumination pattern is often projected using an invisible wavelength such as to not interfere with any accompanying passive camera sensors. Commercially available structured light sensors, such as the Microsoft Kinect (Figure 2.4), have lead to an explosion in applications that utilise active range finding for 3D reconstruction [256]. The second category of active range-finding sensors are time-of-flight cameras, which, instead of measuring the deformation of a known pattern, recover depth by measuring the round trip time of photons projected from a laser or LED. Light Detection and Ranging (LiDAR) is one of the most common examples of a time-of-flight camera [323]. Many robotic systems, including autonomous vehicles, utilise LiDAR as a key component for localisation and mapping, which is known as Simultaneous Localisation and Mapping (SLAM) [352].

Active range-finding sensors usually only recover partial 3D shapes in the form of depth images, but full 3D surfaces can also be estimated by employing either multiple cameras or sequences of images captured using these devices. Kinect-Fusion [256], is a technique for reconstructing 3D surfaces using an active sensor such as the Microsoft Kinect. The system allows users to create detailed 3D reconstructions of indoor environments under varying lighting conditions, using only the depth data acquired with the sensor. Furthermore, Newcombe *et al.* [256] show that through using a GPU and Truncated Signed Distance Field representation, it is possible to achieve real-time 3D reconstruction from an active sensor.

Figure 2.4: Example of RGB image (Left) and depth map (right) captured from a Microsoft Kinect. Purple box highlights degenerate behaviour with reflectiv surfaces. Images taken from the NYUv2 dataset [254]

While active range-finding cameras are capable of capturing detailed and a curate 3D reconstructions, they have several limitations. Strong background lig sources such as the sun or reflective surfaces, may interfere with the light bein projected from the camera resulting in incorrect or missing estimates (Figure 2. Further interference can also be accrued from other active sensors projecting in the environment on the same wavelength. Weather effects, such as rain or fog, c cause photons to scatter and reflect earlier than anticipated, creating unwant sensor noise. As a result, many robotic platforms may rely on fusing observatio from multiple sensors for localisation, 3D mapping (reconstruction) or detecti tasks [392].

2.1.6   Model-based Reconstruction

When we have some prior knowledge about the kinds of objects or scenes that we are trying to reconstruct, it is possible to use model-based reconstruction techniques. Often, model-based reconstruction methods use low dimensional latent representations of 3D shapes that can be used for downstream tasks. For example, Dame *et al.* [62] introduce a method for in-painting occluded regions of a 3D surface recovered using Structure from Motion/SLAM techniques. First, objects of interest are detected and localised in 3D. Sparse 3D points, that are detected in the initial reconstruction, are then replaced using generated 3D shapes sampled from a learnt latent space. These low dimensional latent spaces are commonly referred to as 3D shape priors. Many methods aim to encapsulate an entire shape category (i.e Human, Car, Horse, Chair) for sampling novel examples [11,363]. However, generating new shapes with varied real world input is a challenging problem for reconstruction. These approaches are typically limited by the shape representation and non-rigid transformations between training samples [334]. For example, surface mesh representations typically require exact point correspondences between samples in the dataset for training the latent space model [334].

One of the main challenges when dealing with 3D shapes is the high-dimensionality of the representation. Due to this, many methods rely on a reduced dimensionality version of the desired shape representation. Commonly, a generative model is then learnt on in this compressed space, to allow for sampling intra- or inter-class variations. Allen *et al.* [11] propose a method for reconstructing partial 3D human meshes from 3D laser scan data. Using a collection of 3D meshes previously scanned and reconstructed, the authors [11] propose to use Principal Component Analysis (PCA) to learn the variations in the visual object of interest. A Gaussian distribution is then formed from the variance terms of the PCA and used to sample and reconstruct new unseen meshes. Unfortunately, the PCA shape space representation is only useful when there is a one to one correspondence between the vertices in the mesh and performs poorly when there are non-rigid transformations.

Another challenge when dealing with 3D shapes is matching the observed surface to the estimated shape. Commonly, re-projection losses are used in a optimisation process to find consistent 3D shapes [112,277]. However, to accurately project a 3D shape and match it with the underlying observation, an accurate 3D pose is required. Therefore, 3D shape estimation/sampling is often combined with the optimisation for the underlying 3D pose. Prisacariu *et al.* [277] present a method for simultaneously performing segmentation, pose estimation and 3D reconstruction using 3D shape priors. Unlike Allen *et al.* [11], they specifically limit their method to single rigid shape categories (e.g., cars). Furthermore, rather than using PCA on 3D surface meshes, they propose to use a truncated Discrete Cosine Transform (DCT) [169] representation of 3D Signed Distance Fields. To create their shape space they train a Gaussian Process-Latent Variable Model (GP-LVM) [194] on the truncated DCT coefficients to allow for sampling intra-class variations. To recover the underlying 3D shape and pose, a reprojection loss is minimised by comparing the ground truth object segmentation and the projection of the estimated 3D shape. The main benefit of the compressed DCT shape space is that it allows for efficiently representing high resolution volumes with significantly less memory usage.

2.2   Learning Representations with Deep Learning

Traditional Computer Vision techniques rely on the utilisation of hand-crafted feature descriptors [18,61,224], which can be applied to tasks such as classification, detection, segmentation, 3D reconstruction, localisation and many others. These methods encode an image or image patch into a fixed length vector representation, which aims to capture "low-level" information about the image (e.g., object boundaries and edges) that can then be used for downstream tasks. However, these feature extractors fail to capture higher level semantic and contextual information. Furthermore, the development of these feature extractors is time consuming and often task specific, limiting the generalisability of the approach.

Unlike traditional feature descriptors, deep learning aims to learn complex and hierarchical feature representations that can be used for a vast number of downstream tasks in a wide variety of fields [106]. Typically, deep learning models are constructed using different variants of Artificial Neural Networks [124, 236, 295], which are optimised in an end-to-end fashion using gradient descent. In Computer Vision, Convolutional Neural Networks (CNN) are used to exploit the spatial structure of images to drastically improve computational efficiency and learn translation invariant feature representations. However, deep learning poses its own set of unique challenges. For example, deep learning models require datasets orders of magnitude larger than previous Machine Learning and Computer Vision approaches, as well as requiring immense amounts of computational resources. A combination of the availability of large volumes of data, as well as the computational performance of General Purpose Graphics Processing Units (GPGPUs), has allowed researchers to address these limitations.

In 2012, Krizhevsky *et al.* [183] showed that it was possible to learn features and classify images with deep Convolutional Neural Networks, outperforming traditional feature extractors and classifiers on the ImageNet dataset [67]. More recently, deep learning in Computer Vision has become ubiquitous, being applied with great success in image/video classification, image segmentation, object detection and many other tasks. The key to the success of deep learning lies in the way the models learn complex feature representations, by hierarchically combining simple low level features, which are learnt directly from a large dataset of exemplar image samples. Moreover, it has become a general framework for representation learning, which has allowed researchers to combine modules and share techniques between sub-fields, leading to a renaissance in all areas of Artificial Intelligence.

Of particular interest to this thesis, deep learning offers a more generalisable and efficient means for single view 3D reconstruction, as it can automatically learn to use multiple monocular cues simultaneously. However, issues with computational efficiency and data scarcity pose significant hurdles to the adoption of these techniques in real world 3D reconstruction pipelines.

2.2.1 Convolutional Neural Networks

Convolutional Neural Networks (CNNs) are a specialised type of Artificial Neural Network (ANN) [124, 236, 295] that is designed to process signals with a grid-like topology, such as 2D images or 3D volumes. When dealing with high-dimensional input data it becomes impractical to use fully connected layers, as layer-wise interactions are computed by a multiplication between a matrix of parameters and a matrix of input values. This results in increasingly large memory and computational requirements as the dimensionality of the input data increases. In contrast, by exploiting the spatial structure of the input data, Convolutional Neural Networks can reduce the number of parameters needed for learning feature representations, thereby reducing the memory and computational requirements. This is achieved by replacing the general matrix multiplication, as used in standard Artificial Neural Networks, with a convolution operation with a kernel size smaller than the input data dimensions. This results in sparse connectivity between layers in the network. As each kernel in the convolutional layer is shared for each position in the signal, the number of parameters can be reduced further, drastically improving performance when compared with the dense matrix multiplication employed by fully connected layers of the ANNs.

The parameter sharing in convolutional layers gives rise to a property called equivariance to translation [106]. Put simply, if a function is equivariant, the output changes in equal proportion to the input of the function. This is a useful property, as feature representations will translate proportionally to the amount of translation of an object in an image. Convolutional layers themselves are not invariant to translations, rotations and scales. When this property is desired for a specific task (e.g., image classification), pooling layers [106] are often incorporated into the network. Pooling layers produce summary statistics at intermediate layers of a network, allowing the representation to become invariant to small translations of the input. Due to their sparse connectivity, parameter sharing and equivariant representation learning abilities, convolutional layers have become a key building block in CNNs developed to solve Computer Vision problems.

2.2.2 Deep Unsupervised Learning

While many machine learning problems can be solved using the standard supervised learning paradigm, they require large amounts of labelled data to train which can be expensive and time consuming to obtain. In 3D reconstruction problems, this is further exacerbated, as collecting ground truth data requires many hours of 3D scanning and/or human artistry for each object or scene. One of the major goals of researchers in Machine Learning has been to create models that are capable of learning generic feature representations from data in a label-free manner (i.e., unsupervised learning). This subsection will discuss the two main approaches for achieving this goal: Generative models and self-supervised learning methods.

Unlike supervised methods, which aim to learn a mapping from an input data point to an output label, generative models aim to model the data distribution directly. There are many reasons for using a generative model, such as the need to create models that can compress the data, to learn complex representations without any labels, or to generate novel data points. Boltzmann Machines (1985) [5,316] were one of the first neural network based generative modelling approaches that were able to learn probability distributions over binary input vectors. Following on from Boltzmann Machines, came the development of Deep Belief Networks (DBNs) [129] which were one of the first non-convolutional deep learning models and helped to ignite the "deep learning renaissance" [106].

More recently, Generative Adversarial Network (GAN) [107] and Variational Autoencoder (VAE) [176] have proven to be successful in modelling various types of data (e.g., images [187,280], text [81], and video [54]). GANs are a category of generative deep learning model, which utilises two competing networks, a generator and a discriminator. The generator and discriminator form a game theoretic competition, where the generator network aims to synthesise "counterfeit" samples from the data distribution and the discriminator attempts to distinguish between the real and counterfeit samples. The two models are then updated iteratively until they reach convergence or some predefined stopping criteria. GANs have been applied to a wide variety of problems, such as synthesising photo-realistic images [28,160,280], in-painting of noisy images [375] and], upscaling of low-resolution images [200]. Moreover, they have also been applied to domains outside of images. For example, GANs have been used to generate 3D volumes [361], synthesise realistic voices [23], and design new molecules for use in pharmaceuticals [41].

On the other hand, VAEs are a type of directed generative model that is trained
maximise the variational lower bound associated with the training data. Unli
GANs, which are designed to synthesise high fidelity samples, VAEs are explici
designed to create good latent representations for downstream tasks. This abil
for learning strong latent representations has lead to a range of different app
cations, including semi-supervised learning [175], reinforcement learning [25
and many others. Of special relevance to this thesis, Kulkarni *et al.* [187] propo
to learn an interpretable disentangled representation of 3D scenes from imag
using a VAE. By modifying this disentangled representation, the authors can
synthesise input images with altered scene attributes, such as rotating objects
altering light positioning.

Alternatively, self-supervised learning has emerged as a way of training mod
without labels, where some aspects of the data provide the supervisory sigr
Self-supervised learning is performed by defining a "proxy loss function" th
forces the model to learn semantic representations for the given dataset in
unsupervised manner. These representations can either be used verbatim or fi
tuned on another, much smaller labelled dataset, thereby reducing the amount
labelled data required. One form of self-supervised learning relies on withhold
part of the data and tasking the model to predict the missing component. I
noising autoencoders [340] and split-brain auto-encoders [382] purposely corr
the input image and assign the model to reconstruct the original image. Noro
and Favaro [259] assign the network to solve a task similar to a Jig-Saw puzz
resulting in classification performance similar to a fully supervised model. Seve
papers [193, 341, 381] have shown that useful representations arise when traini
a model to "colourise" images, resulting in features that can be used for obj
tracking and video segmentation [341].

Unlike image based proxy loss functions that aim to complete missing ch
nels or regions, video based self-supervised learning utilises the strong correlat
between temporally adjacent frames to provide a training signal. The tempo

nature of videos allows for models to learn strong semantic representations by exploiting several physical cues such as gravity, friction and biomechanics [354]. Misra *et al.* [245] define a loss function to train a model by predicting the correct temporal order of a video sequence, comparing correct video sequences and shuffled sequences. Alternatively, Wei *et al.* [354] propose to make use of the "arrow of time" and learn image features by predicting whether or not a video is playing in reverse. Self-supervised methods that leverage the rich source of information provided by video, show promise for allowing researchers to train generalisable models with little or no labelled data.

Due to the multi-view nature of video, it has long been used in Computer Vision for tasks such as 3D reconstruction. Unlike, the proxy loss functions defined to predict missing components in images of video, geometric self-supervised loss functions exploit the geometric relationships found in these data sources. These geometric loss functions are used to train models without ground truth labels to address some of the fundamental problems in Computer Vision, such as estimating depth [94, 101], performing 3D volumetric reconstruction [329, 370] and predicting optical flow from video [217]. Details on how self-supervised learning can be applied to learn geometric representations are discussed in Section 2.3.3

2.3   Deep Learning and Geometry

Geometry has been used throughout the field of Computer Vision and forms the foundation of many traditional methods. However, many of these geometric algorithms require first detecting local image features using hand-crafted feature descriptors, leading to reduced generalisation of these methods. Alternatively, deep learning provides a modular framework capable of learning robust features that are applicable to many problems. Furthermore, many of the existing traditional techniques can be updated to use deep learning feature representations in place of the hand-crafted feature descriptors. This section discusses the progress that has been made on merging traditional geometric computer vision techniques with the representational learning power of deep learning models.

2.3.1 Shape Priors in the Deep Learning Era

One of the challenges of performing 3D reconstruction from single view images is that only partial surfaces can be observed, creating gaps in the recovered surface for occluded regions. To address this, traditional methods leverage 3D shape priors to infill these missing regions [387]. This process involves first learning a latent space of 3D shapes, known as a shape prior [277]. Often, a shape prior is created for each individual category of object (e.g. cars, boats, chairs) to learn intra-class variations and requires correctly classifying the object under observation. A shape is then sampled from the corresponding shape prior to incorporate any distinguishing instance level details. To accurately match the sampled 3D shape with the observed image, an optimisation process is often employed. However, these methods typically rely on traditional feature descriptors [277, 336] which are difficult to develop and often fail to generalise to real world situations. By replacing traditional models and feature descriptors with deep learning, we can learn representations that are better suited for 3D reconstruction with the joint modelling of images and shapes. This results in more accurate reconstructions and a greatly simplified reconstruction process.

Wu *et al.* [363] were the first to present a method for 3D reconstruction using deep learning, known as 3D-ShapeNets. Through training a type of generative model called a convolutional deep belief network [129], they were able to reconstruct partial 3D volumes unprojected from a depth map captured from a Microsoft Kinect. Moreover, they use the DBN to show state of the art performance on 3D classification, outperforming hand-crafted volumetric feature descriptors such as the Spherical Harmonic shape descriptor [165] and the Light Field descriptor [40]. Although this work was a large step forward in applying deep learning to 3D reconstruction, the DBN architecture requires a complex training process, leading to sub-optimal results. Additionally, the binary volumetric grid representation used by the authors is expensive in terms of computation and memory usage, limiting the reconstruction to a low-resolution of 30^3 voxels. Finally, the method requires capturing a partial 3D volume from an active range sensor, which is often costly or unavailable.

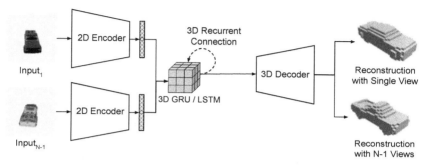

Figure 2.5: Choy *et al.* [52] present 3D-R2N2 which uses a 3D-recurrent module to iteratively perform multi-view volumetric reconstruction using deep learning. Input images take from the ShapeNet dataset [39])

To address the limitations of the 3D-ShapeNets architecture, Choy *et al.* [52] presented 3D-R2N2, a method for volumetric reconstruction from single and multi-view RGB images. Through leveraging newer network architectures and training methodologies, they showed one of the earliest examples of 3D reconstruction directly from images using convolutional neural networks. First, their encoder sub-network converts the image(s) into a feature representation that contains all of the necessary semantic information for reconstruction. Then, the feature representation is transformed into a 3D volume using a series of 3D deconvolution layers in the decoder sub-network. This allows the model to create a mapping between input images and 3D volumes directly, without requiring jointly training a classifier or a complicated sampling of 3D shapes from a separate shape prior model. As the authors aimed to develop both a single and multi-view reconstruction model, they introduced a novel 3D recurrent module, between the encoder and decoder stages, to fuse the feature representations of multiple images (Figure 2.5). More specifically, a 3D Gated Recurrent Unit (GRU) [48] or 3D Long Short Term Memory (LSTM) [132] is trained to fuse multiple view points in the latent representation rather than the traditional method of performing volumetric fusion (e.g. KinectFusion [256]) as a post-processing step. They showed that this allows the model to leverage semantic information from training time, improving the predictions even when there is only a single view available during inference.

While the results of this work are impressive, similarly to 3D-ShapeNets [363], the simple binary volumetric representation results in large computational and memory inefficiencies, limiting the method to coarse reconstructions of 32^3 voxels. One of the aims of this thesis is to address these inefficiencies when working with volumetric representations in the deep learning framework. Furthermore, 3D-ShapeNets and 3D-R2N2 both require large amounts of labelled training data in the form of images to 3D volumes, which can be costly to acquire, often requiring many hours of human artistry per object. Therefore, this thesis also aims to develop self-supervised methods for training single view 3D reconstruction systems using deep learning, with no ground truth 3D shapes.

2.3.2 Learning to Estimate Depth

With the commercial introduction of the Microsoft Kinect and other similar devices, the focus on 3D reconstruction has shifted towards the use of depth sensing technology to improve reconstruction results [255, 256]. While these active range finding based techniques can result in excellent reconstructions, these depth sensing technologies have limits. For example, devices such as Kinect do not perform well in outdoor environments due to Infra-red interference or limited range. Additionally, in many real world applications, a full 3D surface is not required for scene understanding and many existing cameras do not include depth sensors To address this issue, there has been significant research into estimating depth directly from monocular RGB images [73, 74, 94, 101, 304].

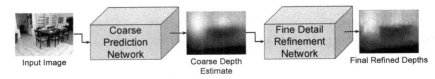

Figure 2.6: Eigen *et al.* [74] propose to use a coarse to fine refinement network for estimating depth from monocular images. Image from NYUv2 Dataset test set [254].

Eigen *et al.* [74], proposed the first deep learning based method for estimating depth from RGB images, showing state of the art results and excellent generalisation when compared with traditional methods [304] (Figure 2.6). The authors train two CNN stacks, one for global coarse grained depth and a second for refining local depth fine grained details, and supervise their model using ground truth RGB-D images captured from a Microsoft Kinect. While these results were excellent at the time of publication, the network architecture in [74] was initially designed to be memory efficient by training the network stacks in two separate stages, and is now considered sub-optimal. Newer papers have instead found that architectures similar to those used in semantic segmentation give significantly improved results with both supervised [88] and self-supervised loss functions [94, 101, 103].

2.3.3 Self-Supervised Learning Meets Geometry

While it is possible to train neural networks to estimate depth from monocular images using training data captured from active range-finding sensors, a persistent challenge for deploying these solutions in the real world is a lack of large and diverse datasets. In practice, capturing these datasets can prove costly. To overcome this, recent works have instead employed self-supervision to learn to estimate depth, reducing the burden of capturing ground truth image sets. Unlike the self-supervised methods discussed earlier in the chapter, geometry based self-supervised learning does not require any fine-tuning as the geometric losses force the model to implicitly learn the task of interest.

By using a loss function based on the photometric image reprojection of synchronized stereo pairs, Garg *et al.* [94] demonstrated that it is possible to train a model to learn to predict disparity (and consequently depth) from monocular images without any ground truth depth images. The photometric reprojection loss is computed by warping the right image of the stereo pair (with a differentiable bilinear sampler [147]) into the left image using the estimated depth. A pixel-wise reconstruction loss can then be computed between the warped image and left image. To improve upon this approach, Godard *et al.* [101] modified the photometric

reprojection loss to penalise depth inconsistencies *bidirectionally* between both le
to right and right to left image pairs.

While these methods were capable of estimating depth for monocular images, the
still required synchronized stereo training data, limiting the practicality of ca
turing large and diverse datasets. This motivated the development of techniqu
that perform self-supervision between frames of a monocular video. Howev
utilising monocular video introduced challenges that were not present when p
forming stereo self-supervision. Unlike for the stereo case, a monocular vid
based photometric reprojection loss also requires accurate relative poses betwe
the frames being warped. To address this issue, Zhou *et al.* [388] proposed
jointly learn to estimate depth and relative pose via the photometric reprojecti
loss. This approach assumes that the only motion present is camera motion as
the scene under observation is static (i.e rigid), however, in practice this is rare
the case and degenerate results emerged due to image sequences that violated th
assumption. To deal with this, Godard *et al.* [103] proposed to include a maski
term that ignores regions violating the rigidity assumption. The authors [103] al
improved upon these results by including a multi-scale estimation and enhanc
photometric reprojection loss function (Figure 2.7). While many improvemer
have been made, monocular self-supervision for depth estimation is still infer.
to binocular self-supervised and fully supervised methods.

Figure 2.7: Monodepth 2 – Godard *et al.* [103] propose to modify the photom
ric reprojection error to improve handing of non-rigid motion when perfoi
ing monocular self-supervised training of depth estimators. Image is modifi
(cropped) from [185] and is licensed under the creative commons 2.0 CC BY
license.

Self-supervision has also been applied to learn model-based 3D reconstructions. Yan *et al.* [370] demonstrated the ability to reconstruct low resolution 3D volumes of objects solely from sequences of image silhouettes. This is performed in a similar manner to the self-supervised depth estimators, where the network first predicts a 3D volume for the given input image and is then projected into a series of 2D occupancy masks. Finally, a reprojection loss is computed against the ground truth silhouettes. However, while object silhouettes are useful as a monocular cue, complex shapes can be difficult to reconstruct accurately as these methods are at best only able to recover the texture-less visual hull of the observed shape. While techniques like self-supervision offer great promise in allowing researchers to train models without any ground truth labels, more research is still required to improve these techniques as they are not as accurate as their supervised counterparts. In this thesis we aim to address several existing challenges when using self-supervision for depth estimation and 3D object reconstruction.

CHAPTER 3

Methodology

This chapter discusses the methodology and definitions used in this thesis. Section 3.1 describes the techniques used in Chapter 4. More specifically, it discusses the Discrete Cosine Transform and how its application can be used to perform 3D volumetric deep learning via our novel IDCT layer. Sec. 3.2 discusses the methodology applied in Chapter 5, including the fundamentals of how self-supervised learning for monocular depth estimation and novel view synthesis can be applied to perform unsupervised 3D point cloud reconstruction. Section 3.2 also includes an overview of the Generative Adversarial Networks framework for novel view synthesis and metrics used to quantify novel view synthesis and point cloud quality. Finally, Section 3.3 defines the components and losses used to achieve state of the art results on KITTI 2015 [95] in Chapter 6. These definitions include 2D Self-Attention, the Discrete Disparity Volume and the improved losses that are used to improve monocular self-supervised depth estimation.

3.1 Efficient Volumetric Reconstruction with Deep Learning

While there has been much success applying deep learning to images and text, developing representation learning algorithms for 3D volumetric data poses many challenges. Chiefly, memory and computational requirements are both increased by an order of magnitude over the standard 2D convolutional neural networks used for images. In Chapter 4, we propose to replace the standard 3D deconvolu tional decoder, used by previous works, with a decoding layer based on the Inverse Discrete Cosine Transform (IDCT). We apply our model, which utilises the IDCT layer to perform single view 3D volumetric reconstruction on the ShapeNet [39] and PASCAL VOC 3D+ [365] datasets. We show that our IDCT decoder is significantly more computationally and memory efficient when compared with deconvolutional decoders, with no loss of accuracy. Furthermore, the improved efficiency allows for training models with an order of magnitude larger volumetric resolution. This section will discuss in more detail the methodology used to create and train a neural network with the Inverse Discrete Cosine layer.

3.1.1   Discrete Cosine Transform

The Discrete Cosine Transform (DCT) is a linear transformation that expresses a finite sequence of data points as the sum of cosine functions, at different frequencies. DCT has found many applications in signal processing, Computer Vision and data compression. In particular, DCT has enabled highly efficient encoding algorithms for both lossless and lossy compression of audio, images and video.

The DCT-II algorithm is the most common variant of DCT, where the 1D frequency domain discrete signal is defined for a 1D time domain discrete signal $f_I(x)$, for $x \in \{0, ..., N-1\}$, as:

$$C_I(u) = \sqrt{\frac{2}{N}} \sum_{x=0}^{N-1} \Lambda(u) f_I(x) \cos\left[\frac{\pi}{N}\left(x+\frac{1}{2}\right)u\right], \qquad (3.1)$$

where $f_I(x)$ is the input signal at a given index x, $C_I(u)$ is the output at coefficient index $u \in \{0, \cdots, N-1\}$, and $\Lambda(u)$ is used along with the scaling factor $\sqrt{\frac{2}{N}}$ to make the transformation and the resulting cosine basis functions orthogonal. In (3.1), $\Lambda(u)$ is defined as

$$\Lambda(u) = \begin{cases} \frac{1}{\sqrt{2}}, & \text{if } u = 0 \\ 1, & \text{otherwise} \end{cases}. \qquad (3.2)$$

A signal can be converted back to the time domain from the frequency domain using the DCT-III algorithm. As DCT-III is the inverse of DCT-II, it is often called the Inverse DCT or simply IDCT. The IDCT converts the cosine basis functions $C_I(u)$, back into the original signal $f_I(x)$ as:

$$f_I(x) = \sqrt{\frac{2}{N}} \sum_{u=0}^{N-1} \Lambda(x) C_I(u) \cos \left[\frac{\pi}{N} \left(u + \frac{1}{2} \right) x \right],$$ (3.3)

where $x \in \{0, \cdots, N-1\}$ and as defined in (3.2), $\Lambda(k)$ is used along with the scaling factor $\sqrt{\frac{2}{N}}$ to make the transformation orthogonal.

3.1.2 Multi-Dimensional Discrete Cosine Transform

The DCT can be applied to a signal with an arbitrary number of dimensions. The Multi-Dimensional DCT (MD-DCT) is achieved by applying the 1D DCT independently across each dimension. Therefore, the DCT-II for a data source $\mathbf{x} \in \mathbb{R}^{N_1 \times N_2 \times N_3}$ is given by:

$$C_{III}(u, v, w) = \sqrt{\frac{2}{N}} \sum_{x=0}^{N_1-1} \sum_{y=0}^{N_2-1} \sum_{z=0}^{N_3-1} f_{III}(x, y, z) \times \Lambda(u) \Lambda(v) \Lambda(w)$$

$$\left\{ \cos \left[\frac{\pi}{N_1} \left(x + \frac{1}{2} \right) u \right] \cos \left[\frac{\pi}{N_2} \left(y + \frac{1}{2} \right) v \right] \cos \left[\frac{\pi}{N_3} \left(z + \frac{1}{2} \right) w \right] \right\},$$ (3.4)

where $k_1 \in \{0, 1, 2, \ldots, N_1 - 1\}$, $k_2 \in \{0, 1, 2, \ldots, N_2 - 1\}$ and $k_3 \in \{0, 1, 2, \ldots, N_3 - 1\}$. Similarly to the IDCT (DCT-III), the inverse MD-DCT is defined as:

$$f_{III}(x, y, z) = \sqrt{\frac{2}{N}} \sum_{u=0}^{N_1-1} \sum_{v=0}^{N_2-1} \sum_{w=0}^{N_3-1} C_{III}(u, v, w) \times \Lambda(x) \Lambda(y) \Lambda(z)$$

$$\left\{ \cos \left[\frac{\pi}{N_1} \left(u + \frac{1}{2} \right) x \right] \cos \left[\frac{\pi}{N_2} \left(v + \frac{1}{2} \right) y \right] \cos \left[\frac{\pi}{N_3} \left(w + \frac{1}{2} \right) z \right] \right\}.$$ (3.5)

3.1.3 Matrix DCT

There exist many implementations of the DCT, which are often based on the Fast Cosine Transform, a derivative of the Fast Fourier Transform [285]. However, to integrate this into a neural network would require implementing efficient GPU kernels for both the forward and backward passes of the model. Instead, we opt to use the matrix formulation of the DCT and IDCT. Based on Eq. 3.3, the 1D-DCT coefficient column vector $\mathbf{C_I} = (C_I(0), C_I(1), \cdots, C_I(N-1))^T$ can be computed in matrix form as

$$\mathbf{C_I} = \mathbf{A_1 f}, \tag{3.6}$$

where $\mathbf{f} = (f(0), f(1), \cdots, f(N-1))^T$ is a column vector containing the discrete signal to be encoded and $\mathbf{A_1} \in \mathbb{R}^{N_1 \times N_1}$ is a cosine basis matrix with entries defined by

$$a_1(u, x) = \Lambda(u) \cos \left[\frac{\pi}{N} \left(x + \frac{1}{2} \right) u \right], \tag{3.7}$$

where $u, x \in \{0, ..., N_1 - 1\}$ – we also denote this matrix with $\mathbf{A_1} = (a_1(u, x))_{N_1 \times N_1}$, and use a similar representation for other matrices defined below. The IDCT is defined in matrix form as

$$\mathbf{f} = \mathbf{A_1}^{-1} \mathbf{C_I}. \tag{3.8}$$

Similarly, the 2D coefficient matrix $\mathbf{C_{II}} = (C_{II}(u, v))_{N_1 \times N_2}$ for a 2D signal $\mathbf{F} = (f_{II}(x, y))_{N_1 \times N_2}$, with $\mathbf{A_2} \in \mathbb{R}^{N_2 \times N_2}$ is formulated as:

$$\mathbf{C_{II}} = \mathbf{A_1 F A_2}^T, \tag{3.9}$$

where $\mathbf{A_2} = (a_2(u, x)_{N_2 \times N_2})$ is the cosine basis matrix with entries defined by:

$$a_2(v, y) = \Lambda(v) \cos \left[\frac{\pi}{N} \left(y + \frac{1}{2} \right) v \right], \tag{3.10}$$

where $v, y \in \{0, ..., N_1 - 1\}$ and $\mathbf{F}$ is the original 2D signal. The 2D IDCT can then be written as:

$$\mathbf{F} = \mathbf{A_1}^{-1} \mathbf{C_{II}} (\mathbf{A_2^T})^{-1}. \tag{3.11}$$

However, as the DCT basis functions are orthonormal, this can be simplified as

$$\mathbf{F} = \mathbf{A_1}^T \mathbf{C_{II}} \mathbf{A_2}. \tag{3.12}$$

Finally, the 3D-DCT can be composed of a succession of 2D-DCT and 1D-DCT operations. Given a three-order tensor $\mathbb{F}_{III} = (f_{III}(x, y, z))_{N_1 \times N_2 \times N_3}$ containing the 3D signal and the cosine basis matrices $\mathbf{A_1}$, $\mathbf{A_2}$ and $\mathbf{A_3} \in \mathbb{R}^{N_3 \times N_3}$, the 3D coefficient matrix $\mathbf{C_{III}} = (C_{III}(u, v, w))_{N_1 \times N_2 \times N_3}$ is mathematically represented using an *n-mode* product [180] as

$$\mathbf{C_{III}} = \mathbb{F}_{III} \times_1 \mathbf{A_1} \times_2 \mathbf{A_2} \times_3 \mathbf{A_3} \tag{3.13}$$

where $\mathbb{F}_{III} \times_1 \mathbf{A}_{1\,j \times n_2 \times n_3} = \sum_{n_1=0}^{N_1} f_{III}(n_1, n_2, n_3))a_1(j, n_1)$ for the first axis, and similarly for the other terms in the *n-mode* product.

The entries for the third cosine basis matrix $\mathbf{A}_3 = (a_3(w, z)_{N_3 \times N_3})$ are defined by

$$a_3(w, z) = \Lambda(w) \cos\left[\frac{\pi}{N}\left(z + \frac{1}{2}\right)w\right] \tag{3.14}$$

where $w, z \in \{0, ..., N_1 - 1\}$. Similarly, the 3D-IDCT is computed as

$$\mathbb{F}_{III} = \mathbf{C}_{III} \times_1 \mathbf{A}_1^{-1} \times_2 \mathbf{A}_2^{-1} \times_3 \mathbf{A}_3^{-1} \tag{3.15}$$

and since $\mathbf{A}_k (1 \leq k \leq 3)$ is orthonormal, this can be simplified as

$$\mathbb{F}_{III} = \mathbf{C}_{III} \times_1 \mathbf{A}_1^T \times_2 \mathbf{A}_2^T \times_3 \mathbf{A}_3^T \tag{3.16}$$

3.1.4 DCT Compression

The DCT coefficient matrix stores the low frequency/high energy information towards the top left, while high frequency/low energy signals are stored toward the bottom right. For sparse signals, such as 3D volumes or 2D images, much of the the high frequency information does not impact the perceptual quality of a reconstructed signal. Therefore, given a DCT coefficient matrix $\mathbf{C}_{II} \in \mathbb{R}^{N_1 \times N}$ for a 2D signal $\mathbf{F} = (f_{II}(x, y))_{N_1 \times N_2}$, we can compress the signal by selecting sub-matrix corresponding to the top K coefficients, in each dimension, where K a hyper-parameter selected ahead of time. The compressed signal $\hat{\mathbf{C}}_{II} \in \mathbb{R}^{K \times K}$ computed as:

$$\hat{\mathbf{C}}_{II} = \mathbf{C}_{II}(1, 2, \cdots, K; 1, 2, \cdots, K), \tag{3.1}$$

where $K < N_1$ and $K < N_2$. This can be trivially extended to the volumetric ca by selecting the sub-tensor that corresponds to the low-frequency coefficients be preserved.

To decompress the signal, the compressed signal can be zero-padded back the original dimension size, forming $\bar{\mathbf{C}}_{II} \in \mathbb{R}^{N \times N}$, before performing the ID function. For example,

$$
\bar{\mathbf{C}}_{II} = \begin{bmatrix}
\hat{C}_{II}(1,1) & \cdots & \hat{C}_{II}(1,K) & 0 & \cdots & 0 \\
\vdots & \ddots & \vdots & 0 & \ddots & 0 \\
\hat{C}_{II}(K,1) & \cdots & \hat{C}_{II}(K,K) & 0 & \cdots & 0 \\
0 & \cdots & 0 & 0 & \cdots & 0 \\
\vdots & \ddots & \vdots & 0 & \ddots & 0 \\
0 & \cdots & 0 & 0 & \cdots & 0
\end{bmatrix}. \tag{3.18}
$$

The operation in Eq. 3.18 can be represented as a function defined by:

$$
\bar{\mathbf{C}}_{II} = \eth_N(\hat{\mathbf{C}}_{II}), \tag{3.19}
$$

where $\eth_N : \mathbb{R}^{K \times K} \mapsto \mathbb{R}^{N \times N}$.

3.1.5 Inverse DCT Layer

To integrate IDCT with a neural network, the deconvolutional module from the encoder-decoder architecture defined by [53] is replaced with a standard fully connected layer. Rather than predicting a 3D volume directly, the output size of this layer is set to the number of coefficients $H = K^3$ that will be used to reconstruct the volume. The compressed volume is then decompressed using by zero-padding the volume (Eq. 3.18) and performing the 3D-IDCT via a series of tensor-matrix multiplications, as defined by Eq. 3.16. The $IDCT(.)$ function is then formulated as:

$$
IDCT(\mathbf{h}, N) = \eth_N(vec^{-1}(\mathbf{h})) *_{\times_1} \mathbf{A_1}^T \times_2 \mathbf{A_2}^T \times_3 \mathbf{A_3}^T, \tag{3.20}
$$

where $vec^{-1}(.)$ is the inverse of the vectorisation function, reshaping the estimated vectorised coefficients $\mathbf{h} \in \mathbb{R}^H$ into a three-order tensor, and $\mathbf{A}_{1,2,3}$ are the cosine basis matrices defined in Eq. 3.7, 3.10, 3.14.

Instead of using the DCT and regressing directly for the coefficients, we opt to use the IDCT as this allows us to compute the loss function in the spatial domain, rather than the frequency domain. In practice, we use a standard Cross Entropy loss function [106] which we found to result in higher quality reconstructions. Moreover, this formulation opens up the application of these layers to a wider variety of problems. The predicted volume $\mathbf{V}_{pr} \in \mathbb{R}^{N \times N \times N}$ is then computed as as:

$$\mathbf{V}_{pr} = \sigma(IDCT(\mathbf{W}^T \mathbf{h} + \mathbf{b}, N)), \tag{3.21}$$

where $\mathbf{W}$ is matrix containing the weights of the layer, $\mathbf{h} \in \mathbb{R}^H$ is the intermediate representation from the encoder network, $\mathbf{b} \in \mathbb{R}^H$ is the bias vector, σ is the Sigmoid activation function [106], N is the original dimension of the target binary volume $\mathbf{V}$, and $IDCT(.)$ is the composition of zero-padding and 3D-IDCT as defined by Eq. 3.20.

3.1.6 Supervised learning for single view 3D volumetric reconstruction

The single view 3D volumetric reconstruction task consists of learning a function $\mathbf{V} = f_{\theta_f}(\mathbf{I})$ that maps an image to a 3D volume using a dataset $\mathcal{D} = \{\mathbf{I}(n), \mathbf{V}_{gt}(n)\}_{n=1}^{|\mathcal{D}|}$ of ground truth images $\mathbf{I} : \Omega \to \mathbb{R}^3$ and 3D volumes $\mathbf{V} : \Psi \to [0,1]$ where Ω denotes the image lattice and Ψ denotes the volume lattice.

We then minimise a reconstruction loss function $\mathcal{L}_{recon}$ to learn the parameters θ_f of the model by comparing the predicted volume $\mathbf{V}_{pr} = f(\mathbf{I}; \theta_f)$ against the ground truth volume $\mathbf{V}_{gt}$ with

$$\theta_f^* = \arg\min_{\theta_f} \frac{1}{|\mathcal{D}|} \sum_{n=1}^{|\mathcal{D}|} \mathcal{L}_{recon}(\mathbf{V}_{gt}(n), f(\mathbf{I}(n); \theta_f)). \tag{3.22}$$

In Chapter 4, we apply sum of voxel Cross-Entropy loss function as used by our baseline method [53] as our reconstruction loss $\mathcal{L}_{recon}(.)$, formulated as:

$$\mathcal{L}_{recon}(\mathbf{V}_{gt}, \mathbf{V}_{pr}) = \sum_{i,j,k} \{\mathbf{V}_{gt}^{(i,j,k)} \log(\mathbf{V}_{pr}^{(i,j,k)}) + (1 - \mathbf{V}_{gt}^{(i,j,k)}) \log(1 - \mathbf{V}_{pr}^{(i,j,k)})\}, \tag{3.23}$$

where $\mathbf{V}_{pr}^{(i,j,k)} \in [0,1]$ represents the predicted object occupancy probabilities for a given voxel (i,j,k) and $\mathbf{V}_{gt}^{(i,j,k)} \in \{0,1\}$ denotes the label for voxel (i,j,k).

3.1.7   Quantitatively Measuring Volumetric Reconstructions

Similarity to [53], to quantitatively measure the quality of our reconstructions, we employ the volumetric intersection-over-union (IOU), defined by:

$$\text{IoU} = \frac{\sum_{i,j,k}[\mathbb{I}(\mathbf{V}_{pr}^{(i,j,k)} > \tau)\mathbb{I}(\mathbf{V}_{gt}^{(i,j,k)})]}{\sum_{i,j,k}[\mathbb{I}(\mathbf{V}_{pr}^{(i,j,k)} > \tau) + \mathbb{I}(\mathbf{V}_{gt}^{(i,j,k)})]}, \tag{3.24}$$

where τ is the voxelization threshold and $\mathbb{I}(.)$ is the indicator function.

3.2   Novel View Prediction for Self-Supervised Point Cloud Reconstruction

In Chapter 5, we present a framework for 3D point cloud reconstruction from monocular images, which requires no ground truth 3D training data, reducing the need for expensive manual data acquisition. We achieve this by leveraging self-supervised learning techniques for depth estimation [94, 100] and deep generative models [107] for novel view prediction [267]. By combining these two methods, we show how it is possible to reconstruct high quality 3D textured point clouds using only images for training. This section covers the methodology used to train both self-supervised depth estimators and novel view prediction models.

3.2.1   Novel View Synthesis

Novel view synthesis is the task of generating or synthesising new unseen view points of an object or scene. Typically, this takes the form of training a model $\mathbf{I}_b = g(\mathbf{I}_a; \theta_g)$ to learn a mapping between an input image $\mathbf{I}_a$ and a new view of the scene or object $\mathbf{I}_b$, using a dataset of ground truth view points $\mathcal{D} = \{(\mathbf{I}_a(n), \mathbf{I}_b(n))\}_{n=0}^{|\mathcal{D}|}$. The simplest way of achieving this is to train the model to minimise a simple reconstruction style loss, such as a Mean Squared Error (MSE) or Mean Absolute Error (MAE), as follows:

$$\theta_g^* = \arg\min_{\theta_g} \frac{1}{|\mathcal{D}|} \sum_{n=1}^{|\mathcal{D}|} \mathcal{L}_{recon}(\mathbf{I}_b(n), g(\mathbf{I}_a(n); \theta_g)). \tag{3.25}$$

In Chapter 5 we opt to use the MAE as our reconstruction term, defined as:

$$\mathcal{L}_{recon}(\mathbf{I}_b, g(\mathbf{I}_a; \theta_g)) = \|\mathbf{I}_b - g(\mathbf{I}_a; \theta_g)\|_1. \tag{3.26}$$

While simple reconstruction loss functions encourage the model to synthesise images that are consistent with the original object or scene, they often result in blurry images. As the quality of our 3D reconstructions is dependent on not only the depth estimation model, but also the quality of the synthesised images, we opt to train our novel view model using a generative adversarial loss function [107, 267], to further improve visual fidelity, which will be discussed in the following section.

3.2.2 Generative Adversarial Networks

Generative Adversarial Networks (GAN) [107] have emerged as an effective method for deep generative modelling, due to the high fidelity samples they can produce. As discussed in Chapter 2, GAN training is formulated as a game theoretic competition between a generator network $g(.)$ and an adversary discriminator $d(.)$. The goal of GANs is to learn how to generate new samples from an underlying latent distribution, represented by $p_{data}(\mathbf{x})$, of the training data $\mathcal{D} = \{\mathbf{x}(n)\}_{n=1}^{|\mathcal{D}|}$. To achieve this, it learns a mapping from input noise samples $\mathbf{z} \sim p_\mathbf{z}(\mathbf{z}) = \mathcal{N}(\mathbf{z}; \mu, \Sigma)$, generated from a normal distribution of mean μ and covariance Σ, to the input data points $\mathbf{x}$. While the discriminator $d(\mathbf{x})$ outputs a scalar representing the probability that $\mathbf{x}$ came from the data distribution $p_{data}(\mathbf{x})$ rather than from the generator distribution $p_g(\mathbf{x})$. Put simply, the generator and discriminator engage in a minimax game where, the generator attempts to synthesise fake samples, while the discriminator tries to identify the forgeries. Mathematically, this is defined as:

$$\min_g \max_d \mathcal{L}_{gan}(d, g), \tag{3.27}$$

where $\mathcal{L}_{gan}(d, g) = \mathbb{E}_{x \sim p_{data}(\mathbf{x})}[log(d(\mathbf{x}))] + \mathbb{E}_{\mathbf{z} \sim p_z(\mathbf{z})}[log(1 - d(g(\mathbf{z})))]$. While useful for generating random images or 3D volumes, the unconditional GAN cannot sample specific object categories or instances. However, the GAN framework can be altered to become a conditional generative model $p_g(\mathbf{x}|\mathbf{y})$ by adding a conditioning vector $\mathbf{y}$ as input to both $g(.)$ and $d(.)$ [107, 244, 261]. The standard conditional GAN [244] (cGAN) is defined as follows:

$$\min_{g} \max_{d} \mathcal{L}_{cgan}(d,g), \tag{3.28}$$

where $\mathcal{L}_{cgan}(d,g) = \mathbb{E}_{\mathbf{x} \sim p_{data}(\mathbf{x}|\mathbf{y})}[log(d(\mathbf{x}|\mathbf{y}))] + \mathbb{E}_{\mathbf{z} \sim p_{z}(\mathbf{z}|\mathbf{y})}[log(1 - d(g(\mathbf{z}|\mathbf{y})))].$

3.2.3 Novel View Synthesis with Conditional Generative Adversarial Networks

As cGANs were initially developed to perform category level sampling of images, they need to be modified to perform the instance level novel view synthesis that we require. To achieve this several changes need to be made to the traditional generator and discriminator network architectures. Firstly, the generator needs to be modified to include an encoder network, for example, by using a network architecture such as the UNet [293]. Secondly, the discriminator architecture needs to be modified to be conditioned on images rather than class labels. This is realized by simply concatenating the ground truth images channel-wise to the existing image batches.

Empirically, we found that that the standard conditional adversarial loss [107] (Eq. 3.28) was unstable, often leading to degenerate images due to mode collapse. Alternatively, we found that the the least squares generative adversarial loss (LS-GAN) [230] formulation, showed significantly more stable results during training. In practice, the generator and discriminator are optimised in an alternating fashion, requiring independent weight updates for each network. Therefore, the LSGAN loss functions for the discriminator network $d(.)$ is defined by:

$$\mathcal{L}_{dis}(g,d) = \frac{1}{2}\mathbb{E}[(d(\mathbf{I}_b) - 1)^2] + \frac{1}{2}\mathbb{E}[(d(g(\mathbf{I}_a))^2], \tag{3.29}$$

where $\mathbf{I}_a$ is the input image and $\mathbf{I}_b$ is the ground truth image(s) for each of the novel viewpoints we wish to synthesise for the scene depicted $\mathbf{I}_a$. The loss function for the generator network $g(.)$ is defined as:

$$\mathcal{L}_{gen}(g,d) = \mathbb{E}[(d(g(\mathbf{I}_a)) - 1)^2]. \tag{3.30}$$

Until recently, one of the major challenges with Generative Adversarial Networks was generating high resolution images greater than 128x128. One of the proposed solutions to this problem, was to use multiple discriminator networks at varying image scales. This was was shown [141,345] to improve the both local and global consistency, resulting in higher fidelity images. As we wish to generating high quality point clouds from the novel view images, we apply three discriminators at three different scales, represented by $d_k(.)$ where $k \in \{1,2,3\}$. The multiple discriminator loss, is now modified to optimise the sum of each of the discriminator losses (Eq. 3.29) for each scale k, as in

$$\mathcal{L}_{msdis} = \sum_{k=1,2,3} \mathcal{L}_{dis}(g, d_k). \tag{3.31}$$

The multi-scale generator loss, is also adapted to use the sum of the generato losses (Eq. 3.30) for each discriminator scale k.

$$\mathcal{L}_{msgen} = \sum_{k=1,2,3} \mathcal{L}_{gen}(g, d_k), \tag{3.32}$$

To further improve training stability and results we also apply an adversaria feature matching loss [267,345]. To compute the feature matching loss, featur representations are extracted from discriminator at multiple feature scales, fc both the synthesised images and ground truth image batches. The $L1$ error is the computed between matching sets of ground truth and synthesised feature ma As we have multiple discriminators, our feature matching loss extracts multip feature maps from the different scales discriminators $d_k(.)$, as follows:

$$\mathcal{L}_{feat}(g, d_k) = \sum_{t=0}^{T} \frac{1}{N_t} \|d_k^{(t)}(\mathbf{I}_y) - d_k^{(t)}(g(\mathbf{I}_x))\|_1, \tag{3.3}$$

where T represents the number of intermediate layers to extract feature maps. T error between the feature maps is then weighted by the size of each feature m N_t at each intermediate feature t. The multi-scale feature matching loss, using t discriminators $d_k(.)$ as

$$\mathcal{L}_{msfeat} = \sum_{k=1,2,3} \mathcal{L}_{feat}(g, d_k). \tag{3.}$$

Finally, to encourage consistent reconstructions, we incorporate a reconstruction loss (Eq. 3.26) to the cGAN loss. The final generator loss is then defined as a weighted sum of the multi-scale generator loss (Eq. 3.32), multi-scale feature matching loss (Eq. 3.33) and reconstruction loss reconstruction loss (Eq. 3.26):

$$\mathcal{L}_{gen}(g,d) = \mathcal{L}_{recon} + \lambda_1 \mathcal{L}_{msfeat} + \lambda_2 \mathcal{L}_{msgen}, \tag{3.35}$$

where λ_1 and λ_2 represent the weighting terms for each component.

Typically, when training GANs, $d(.)$ tends to converge faster than $g(.)$. This leads to many strategies for when to switch between training $d(.)$ and $g(.)$. We apply the two timescale update rule (TTUR) [127], when training $d(.)$ and $g(.)$. Instead of switching the training every n^{th} batch, the TTUR instead uses two separate learning rates for the generator and the discriminator models. Typically, the learning rate for the discriminator is set to be higher than that of the generator. This simplifies the training algorithm and allows us to update $d(.)$ and $g(.)$ for every batch when performing stochastic gradient decent. The TTUR improves the training dynamics of the adversarial training, thereby improving the chances of reaching Nash Equilibrium.

3.2.4   Self-Supervised Depth Estimation

To convert the synthesised novel view images into 3D point clouds, we use a depth estimation model $z : I \rightarrow Z$ which maps an input image $I : \Omega \rightarrow \mathbb{R}^3$ to a depth image $Z : \Omega \rightarrow \mathbb{R}$ which is trained using self-supervision. The main benefit of training depth estimators using self-supervision is that it requires no ground truth depth or 3D data – it instead relies on binocular images or monocular video to provide the supervision. Self-supervised depth estimation networks are trained by warping a source image I_b into a target image I_a, using the predicted depths and known relative poses $T \in \mathbb{R}^{4 \times 4}$, and applying a photometric re-projection error (Sec. 3.2.5). The target image I_a is first processed by a Convolutional Neural Network to produce a disparity/depth estimate $Z_a : \Omega \mapsto \mathbb{R}$ for each pixel in I_a. The relative 3D rigid transformation matrix between source and target frames

$\mathbf{T}_{b \mapsto a} \in \mathbb{R}^{4 \times 4}$ and the camera intrinsics matrix $\mathbf{K}$ are then used to re-project the source frame into the target frame.

The rigid transformation matrix $\mathbf{T}_{b \mapsto a}$ can be represented in homogeneous coordinates in terms of a rotation matrix and translation vector:

$$\mathbf{T}_{b \mapsto a} = \begin{bmatrix} \mathbf{R}_{b \mapsto a} & \mathbf{t}_{b \mapsto a} \\ 0 & 1 \end{bmatrix}. \tag{3.36}$$

The camera intrinsics $\mathbf{K}$, is parameterized using the focal lengths $f_{x,y}$ and the optical centres $c_{x,y}$ as:

$$\mathbf{K} = \begin{bmatrix} f_x & 0 & c_x \\ 0 & f_y & c_y \\ 0 & 0 & 1 \end{bmatrix}. \tag{3.37}$$

In Chapter 5 we train our models using synthetically rendered objects from the ShapeNet [39] dataset. The focal lengths are converted from the standard OpenGL perspective transformation matrix and we fix the optical centres at the image centre such that $c_x = width/2$ and $c_y = height/2$.

To warp the source frame $\mathbf{I}_b$ into the view point of the target frame $\mathbf{I}_a$, the source frame is first unprojected using the camera intrinsics $\mathbf{K}$ and depth values $\mathbf{Z}_a$ to form a point cloud $\mathbf{P}_a \in \mathbb{R}^{N \times 4}$. The point cloud $\mathbf{P}_b$ is made up of a set of 3D coordinates, where the x and y coordinates $\mathbf{P}_b^{(x)}$ and $\mathbf{P}_b^{(y)}$, are uniformly sampled from a 2D grid between $[-1, 1]$ for each spatial location in $\mathbf{I}_a$, the z coordinate is created by vectorising and unprojecting the depth map $\mathbf{P}_b^{(z)} = \mathbf{K}^{-1} vec(\mathbf{Z}_a)^T$ and the 4th dimension represents the homogeneous coordinate $\mathbf{P}_b^{(w)} = 1$. The unprojected points $\mathbf{P}_b$ are then transformed back into the pose of the target frame using the relative camera pose $\mathbf{T}_{b \mapsto a}$, resulting in the 3D flow field $\mathbf{P}_{b \mapsto a} \in \mathbb{R}^{N \times 4}$ from source to target image. This process is defined as:

$$\mathbf{P}_{b \mapsto a} = \mathbf{K} \mathbf{T}_{b \mapsto a} \mathbf{P}_b^T. \tag{3.38}$$

The pixels in the target image are warped into the source image $\hat{\mathbf{I}}_a$ using the 3D optical flow $\mathbf{P}_{b \mapsto a}$ and a differentiable image sampler $\langle . \rangle$ [147]

$$\hat{\mathbf{I}}_a = \langle (\mathbf{I}_b, \mathbf{P}_{b \mapsto a}) \rangle. \tag{3.39}$$

Finally, to train the model, a photometric reprojection error can be computed and used to optimise the network.

3.2.5   Photometric Reprojection Error

The photometric re-projection error [94, 101] is then computed between the warped source image $\hat{\mathbf{I}}_a$ and the target image $\mathbf{I}_a$ forcing the network to implicitly learn how to estimate depth for monocular images. Therefore, at test time only a single image is required to predict depth. The photometric re-projection loss can be any image reconstruction loss function computed in pixel space such as MSE or MAE. In Chapter 5, we find that using the mean absolute error (i.e., L1 distance) enables more accurate depth estimates than MSE. Mathematically, the photometric reprojection loss function is defined as:

$$\mathcal{L}_{pe} = \|\mathbf{I}_a - \hat{\mathbf{I}}_a\|_1. \tag{3.40}$$

3.2.6   Background Masking and Un-projection

At test time, we chain the novel view synthesis and depth estimation to recover a set of M novel view point images for the observed object. We can then create the final 3D point cloud by un-projecting the RGB-D in a similar manner to the image reprojection process described in Eq. 3.38. The point cloud $\mathbf{P}_m \in \mathbb{R}^{N \times 4}$ for a given view point image $\mathbf{I}_m$, is formed by vectorising, homogenising and unprojecting the depth map $\mathbf{Z}_m$ where m is the index of the image in the set of images M. Similarly to Eq. 3.38, the x and y coordinates are formed by sampling from a uniform 2D grid, between $[-1, 1]$ for each spatial location (i, j) in $\mathbf{Z}_m$ and concatenating with the depth map and homogeneous coordinate to form $\bar{\mathbf{Z}}_m : \Omega \to \mathbb{R}^4$ where $\bar{\mathbf{Z}}_m(i, j) = (x, y, z, 1)$. Then by using the camera intrinsics $\mathbf{K}$ and absolute pose $\mathbf{T}_m$ rather than the relative pose, we can un-project the depths into an aligned and canonicalised 3D point cloud $\mathbf{P} \in \mathbb{R}^{N \times 4}$ using the un-projection function $\psi(.)$ as

$$\mathbf{P} = \psi(\bar{\mathbf{Z}}_m, \mathbf{K}_m, \mathbf{T}_m), \tag{3.41}$$

where the un-projection function is defined as:

$$\psi(\bar{\mathbf{Z}}_m, \mathbf{K}_m, \mathbf{T}_m) = \mathbf{T}_m^{-1}(\mathbf{K}_m^{-1} vec(\bar{\mathbf{Z}}_m)^T), \tag{3.42}$$

where m denotes the index of the novel view, and $vec(\bar{\mathbf{Z}}_m)$ returns an $N \times 4$ matrix of the 4D vectors in the mapping $\bar{\mathbf{Z}}_m$. Each of the image RGB values are then also vectorised and concatenated with the corresponding point locations to form a textured 3D point cloud.

In Chapter 5, we train the models using synthetically rendered images from the ShapeNet [39] with randomly coloured backgrounds. In practice, we found that randomly changing the backgrounds stopped both the adversarial network used in novel view model and depth estimation model over-fitting to the background. However, this poses a problem, in that depth values are still predicted for the background pixels. To address this, we add an additional step for synthetic images. The novel view model is adapted to also predict a binary mask $\mathbf{M}_{bg} : \Omega \mapsto [0, 1]$ for foreground and background pixels, which are then used filter out pixels that are predicted as background after un-projection.

3.2.7 Point Cloud Reconstruction with Novel View Synthesis and Depth Estimation

At test time , the predicted point cloud $\mathbf{P}_{pr} \in \mathbb{R}^{N \times 4}$ can be recovered by composing the novel view prediction with the depth estimator. The single-view input image $\mathbf{I}_a$ is passed through novel view the model $g(.)$, which synthesises a set of V fixed pose novel views $\{\mathbf{I}_v\}_{v=1}^{V} = g(\mathbf{I}_a)$. Depths are then estimated for these novel views images using the previously trained depth estimator $z(.)$ which maps an input image $\mathbf{I} : \Omega \to \mathbb{R}^3$ to a depth image $\mathbf{Z} : \Omega \to \mathbb{R}$ to produce RGB-D images. Finally, the generated images can be un-projected using a modified version of the un-projection function $\psi(.)$ defined in Eq. 3.42, as follows:

$$\mathbf{P}_{pr} = \psi(\{z(\mathbf{I}_v)\}_{v=1}^{V}, \mathbf{K}, \{\mathbf{T}_v\}_{v=1}^{V}), \tag{3.43}$$

where $\mathbf{K} \in \mathbb{R}^{4 \times 4}$ is the camera intrinsics matrices and this version of $\psi(.)$ takes as input a set of corresponding depth maps and transformations instead of a single corresponding depth map and transformation from Eq. 3.42. The textured point cloud $\mathbf{P}_{rgb} \in \mathbf{R}^{N \times 6}$, containing the 3D location and RGB values is formed by vectorising and concatenating the novel view images $\{\mathbf{I}_v\}_{v=1}^{V}$ with the predicted point cloud $\mathbf{P}_{pr}$. Finally, background points are filtered out using the predicted background masks $\mathbf{M}_{bg}$, leaving only points that correspond to the 3D surface of interest.

3.2.8 Quantitatively measuring point cloud reconstructions

In Chapter 5 we utilise the Chamfer Distance (CD) [78] to quantitatively measure the quality of our point cloud reconstructions. Given a ground truth point cloud $\mathbf{P}_{gt}$ and a predicted point cloud $\mathbf{P}_{pr}$, the Chamfer Distance finds the nearest neighbour in the other point set and sums the squared distances. Mathematically, this is defined as:

$$d_{Chamf}\left(\mathbf{P}_{gt}, \mathbf{P}_{pr}\right) = \sum_{\mathbf{x} \in \mathbf{P}_{gt}} \min_{\mathbf{y} \in \mathbf{P}_{pr}} \|\mathbf{x} - \mathbf{y}\|_2^2 + \sum_{\mathbf{y} \in \mathbf{P}_{pr}} \min_{\mathbf{x} \in \mathbf{P}_{gt}} \|\mathbf{x} - \mathbf{y}\|_2^2. \tag{3.44}$$

3.2.9 Quantitatively measuring image quality

In many tasks where the output of a model or algorithm is an image, it is desirable to be able to quantify the quality of the synthesised or reconstructed images. The Structured Similarity image metric (SSIM) [350] is often used as a perceptual measure of quality for comparing two images, a ground truth image $\mathbf{I}$ and a processed or degraded image $\hat{\mathbf{I}}$. Unlike the Mean Squared Error (MSE) or Peak-Signal to Noise Ratio (PSNR), which measure absolute error, SSIM was designed to model the perceptual change in structural information in the image. Due to this, SSIM and its derivatives have found significant utilisation in measuring lossy image compression algorithms. The SSIM metric is computed between the two sets of corresponding image patches $\mathbf{X}$ and $\hat{\mathbf{X}}$ of size $W \times W$ pixels, extracted from the ground truth image $\mathbf{I}$ and the degraded image $\hat{\mathbf{I}}$, respectively, where typically $W = 11$ [350]. SSIM is comprised of three comparison functions which evaluate luminance $l(\hat{\mathbf{X}}, \mathbf{X})$, contrast $c(\hat{\mathbf{X}}, \mathbf{X})$ and structure $s(\hat{\mathbf{X}}, \mathbf{X})$:

$$l(\hat{\mathbf{X}}, \mathbf{X}) = \frac{2\mu_x \mu_{\hat{x}} + c_1}{\mu_x^2 + \mu_{\hat{x}}^2 + c_1}, \tag{3.45}$$

$$c(\hat{\mathbf{X}}, \mathbf{X}) = \frac{2\sigma_x \sigma_{\hat{x}} + c_2}{\sigma_x^2 + \sigma_{\hat{x}}^2 + c_2}, \tag{3.46}$$

$$s(\hat{\mathbf{X}}, \mathbf{X}) = \frac{\sigma_{x\hat{x}} + c_3}{\sigma_x \sigma_{\hat{x}} + c_3}, \tag{3.47}$$

where μ_x and $\mu_{\hat{x}}$ are the means for each window, σ_x and $\sigma_{\hat{x}}$ are the variance for ea
window and $\sigma_{\hat{x}x}$ is the covariance between the windows $\hat{\mathbf{X}}$ and $\mathbf{X}$. The constants
and c_2 are typically set to the accepted values of $c_1 = 0.01^2$ and $c_2 = 0.03^2$, wh
the constant c_3 is defined as $\frac{c_2}{2}$. The SSIM is then the weighted combination of t
three components:

$$SSIM(\hat{\mathbf{X}}, \mathbf{X}) = \left[l(\hat{\mathbf{X}}, \mathbf{X})^\alpha \cdot c(\hat{\mathbf{X}}, \mathbf{X})^\beta \cdot s(\hat{\mathbf{X}}, \mathbf{X})^\gamma \right],$$ (3.4

where α, β and γ are the weighting terms for each component. In the standa
SSIM, $\alpha, \beta, \gamma = 1$ and is therefore reduced to:

$$SSIM(\hat{\mathbf{X}}, \mathbf{X}) = \frac{(2\mu_{\hat{x}}2\mu_x + c_1)(2\sigma_{\hat{x}x} + c_2)}{(\mu_{\hat{x}}^2 + \mu_x^2 + c_1)(\sigma_{\hat{x}}^2 + \sigma_x^2 + c_2)}.$$ (3.

The SSIM measure returns a value in the range $[-1.0, 1.0]$ with 1.0 being a perf
match to the original image and -1.0 indicating no structural similarity. In Chap
5 we use the SSIM metric to measure the quality of various methods for no
view prediction. When used as a whole image metric, the $SSIM$ index is averag
over all of the M extracted image patches and is known as the Mean Structur
Similarity Index (MSSIM). The MSSIM is defined as:

$$MSSIM(\hat{\mathbf{I}}, \mathbf{I}) = \frac{1}{M} \sum_{j=1}^{M} SSIM(\hat{\mathbf{X}}(j), \mathbf{X}(j))),$$ (3.

where j indexes one of the M patches from images $\hat{\mathbf{I}}$ and $\mathbf{I}$.

SSIM can also be converted to measure dissimilarity and be used as a loss functi
for training. The Structured Dissimilarity Loss (DSSIM) is defined as:

$$DSSIM(\hat{\mathbf{X}}, \mathbf{X}) = \frac{1 - SSIM(\hat{\mathbf{X}}, \mathbf{X})}{2}.$$ (3.

We apply the Structured Dissimilarity loss in Chapter 6, as part of a photome
reprojection error, for training self-supervised depth estimators.

3.3 Improving Self-Supervised Depth Estimation

Monocular depth estimation has increasingly becoming one of the most research
areas in Computer Vision. While excellent progress has been made using
pervised learning techniques, capturing large and diverse datasets hinders

development of generalisable models. Therefore, self-supervised depth estimators (Sec. 3.2.4) have emerged as a viable alternative to supervised training approaches by leveraging either synchronised stereo pairs or monocular video rather than ground truth depth images. However, self-supervised depth estimation models still lag behind the accuracy of purely supervised methods. Moreover, having estimates of prediction uncertainty is a valuable addition to depth estimators [166] and has been left unaddressed for the monocular self-supervised case. We investigate these issues in Chapter 6, improving self-supervised depth estimators by applying 2D self-attention and a discrete volumetric representation. Incorporating self-attention into the depth estimator increases the receptive field, adding additional contextual information to the predictions by allowing the network to reason over non-local areas of the image. Not only the discrete disparity volume (DDV) produces robust and sharper depth estimates, they also allow for the computation of per pixel depth uncertainties. In Chapter 6, we show that both of these contributions lead to state of the art results for monocular self-supervised depth estimation on the KITTI 2015 [95] and Make3D [304] datasets. This section will cover the methodology used in that chapter.

3.3.1   Self-Supervised Learning on Monocular Video Sequences

While the initial development of self-supervised depth estimators focused on using synchronised binocular images, large datasets of binocular images are still widely unavailable. Instead, many researchers have turned their attention to monocular video as a source of self-supervision. We represent an RGB image at time t in the sequence, as $\mathbf{I}_t$. However, unlike stereo image pairs, monocular video has an unconstrained pose between frames. To leverage monocular video for self-supervision, we must jointly estimate depth and relative pose between images in the sequence. Similar to other papers [103, 388], we opt to train a second network, the pose estimator, which takes two temporally adjacent images extracted from the video sequence, $\mathbf{I}_t$ and $\mathbf{I}_{t'}$, and returns the relative transformation between them, as in

$$\mathbf{T}_{t' \to t} = p(\mathbf{I}_t, \mathbf{I}_{t'}; \phi), \tag{3.52}$$

where $\mathbf{T}_{t' \to t}$ denotes the transformation matrix between images recorded at time steps t and t', and $p(.; \phi)$ is the pose estimator, consisting of a deep learning model parameterised by ϕ. The estimated relative pose $\mathbf{T}_{t' \to t}$, is then used to warp the source image $\mathbf{I}_{t'}$ into the target image $\mathbf{I}_t$, producing the transformed image $\mathbf{I}_{t' \to t}$. The depth map $\mathbf{D}_t$ is predicted by minimizing the photometric re-projection error (Section 3.2.5) between the source and target images, defined as:

$$\mathcal{L}_{pe} = \sum_t \sum_{t'} pe(\mathbf{I}_t, \mathbf{I}_{t' \to t}), \tag{3.53}$$

where

$$\mathbf{I}_{t' \to t} = \mathbf{I}_{t'} \langle proj(\sigma(\mathbf{D}_t), \mathbf{T}_{t' \to t}, \mathbf{K}) \rangle, \tag{3.54}$$

$pe(.)$ denotes the photometric reconstruction error defined in Eq. 3.61, $proj(.)$ represents the 2D coordinates of the projected depths $\mathbf{D}_t$ in $\mathbf{I}_{t'}$, and $\langle . \rangle$ is the sampling operator.

3.3.2 Self-Attention for Depth Estimation

Self-Attention has been shown to drastically improve performance of natural language processing (NLP) tasks by improving the way in which the networks handle dependencies between words [335]. RNNs [299], LSTMs [132] and CNNs [90,196] only process information in the local neighbourhoods limiting their ability to reason about long range dependencies between tokens in the sequence. Similarly in Computer Vision, Wang *et al.* [347] were inspired by non-local means [34], to develop a 2D self-attention layer that computes feature responses at a specified position as the weighted sum of all features at all positions in the input feature map. In contrast to standard convolutional layers, the self-attention layers capture long-range dependencies by directly computing interactions between spatial positions in a feature map regardless of the positional distance [347]. As standard convolutions may struggle to model contextual relationships between non-contiguous regions, we hypothesise that it is possible to improve monocular depth estimation by incorporating non-local aggregation strategies, such as 2D Self-Attention.

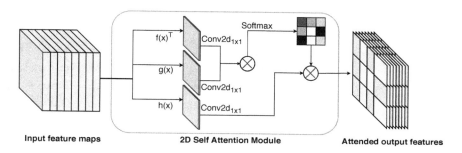

Figure 3.1: Overview of the 2D Self-Attention module.

The input to the self-attention model is the feature representations $\mathbf{X} = resnet_\theta(\mathbf{I}_t)$ encoded from the input image $\mathbf{I}_t$ using a ResNet [123] encoder $resnet_\theta$, with $\mathbf{X} : \Omega_{1/8} \rightarrow \mathbb{R}^C$, C representing the number of output channels used in the encoder, and $\Omega_{1/8}$ denoting the low-resolution lattice at $(1/8)^{th}$ of its original resolution in Ω. The encoded features $\mathbf{X}$ are then used to compute the query $f(\mathbf{X})$, they key $g(\mathbf{X})$ and value $h(\mathbf{X})$ components represented by:

$$
\begin{aligned}
f(\mathbf{X}(i,j)) &= \mathbf{W}_f \mathbf{X}(i,j), \\
g(\mathbf{X}(i,j)) &= \mathbf{W}_g \mathbf{X}(i,j), \\
h(\mathbf{X}(i,j)) &= \mathbf{W}_h \mathbf{X}(i,j),
\end{aligned}
\tag{3.55}
$$

with the weights for each layer $\mathbf{W}_f, \mathbf{W}_g, \mathbf{W}_h \in \mathbb{R}^{N \times M}$. In practice, three separate 1×1 convolutions are applied to efficiently compute each component. The attention matrices $\mathbf{S}_{ij} : \Omega_{1/8} \rightarrow [0,1]$ are then computed by applying a $softmax(.)$ over the query and key:

$$
\mathbf{S}_{i,j} = softmax(f(\mathbf{X}(i,j))^T g(\mathbf{X})),
\tag{3.56}
$$

The final self-attention values are formed by multiplying $\mathbf{S}_{ij}$ in (3.56) with the value of the feature representation $h(\mathbf{X})$ as defined by:

$$
\mathbf{A}(i,j) = \sum_{\tilde{i},\tilde{j} \in \Omega_{1/8}} h(\mathbf{X}(\tilde{i},\tilde{j})) \times \mathbf{S}_{i,j}(\tilde{i},\tilde{j}),
\tag{3.57}
$$

where $\mathbf{A} : \Omega_{1/8} \rightarrow \mathbb{R}^N$.

3.3.3 Discrete Disparity Volume

Traditional stereo or depth estimation algorithms often utilise a discrete cost/probability volume to regularise and regress depth or disparity. However, representations like discrete volumes pose three challenges. Firstly, 3D convolution is expensive as compute and memory usage grows cubically with the size of the volume. Secondly, they are not differential and able to be trained via back-propagation when used implicitly as part of a self-supervised depth estimator. Finally, they are unable to produce sub-voxel estimates, limiting reconstruction accuracy.

As occluded objects or regions are not visible when performing monocular depth estimation, each ray along the depth dimension is independent from one another. Therefore, as occluded regions cannot contribute to the final outcome, it is unnecessary to convolve along the disparity/depth dimension as well as the spatial dimensions. To address the issue of computational complexity, we propose to apply a 2D Convolution with K output channels, rather than the traditional 3D convolution. This drastically improves computational and memory efficiency, while retaining the regularisation effect benefited by the volumetric representation.

While in the supervised case it is possible to use discrete depth values [88], using discrete depths for self-supervised learning results in quantization artefacts which will adversely affect the performance of the photometric reprojection loss. Moreover, using discrete depths requires projecting the discrete volume probabilities to into a depth image by taking an *argmax* over the depth ray prior to applying the photometric reprojection error. As the *argmax* operation is not differentiable, we propose to use a softargmax function, also sometimes called soft-attention. The output probability volume **D** is normalised by a softmax operation and multiplied by the positional encoding *disparity*(k) that contains K evenly spaced samples calculated over the interval [$depth_{min}, depth_{max}$], where each element is defined by

$$disparity(k) = \left[depth_{min} + k \left(\frac{depth_{max} - depth_{min}}{K-1} \right) \right],$$ (3.58)

where $k \in \{0, \cdots, K-1\}$. By encoding the depth in this manner, it is possible to both regress sub-voxel disparity estimates, while also allowing us to constrain and regularise the disparity values. The probabilities are then summed along each ray to project the volume into a disparity image $\sigma(\mathbf{D})(i,j)$ for pixel location $(i,j) \in \mathbb{N}^{H \times W}$. Mathematically, this is defined as:

$$\sigma(\mathbf{D}(i,j)) = \sum_{k=0}^{K} softmax(\mathbf{D}(i,j)[k]) \times disparity(k) \qquad (3.59)$$

where $softmax(\mathbf{D}(i,j)[k])$ represents the softmax result of the kth element along the depth axis of the 3D volume $\mathbf{D}$ at the image position (i,j). As noted by [168], when comparing with the argmax operator, the final disparity can be influenced by all values and therefore be susceptible to multi-modal distributions. To address this, in the Convolution prior to the *softargmax* operation, we omit Batch-Normalisation [144] so that the network can learn to control the *temperature* of the softmax and scale the disparity probabilities directly.

3.3.4 Multi-scale Discrete Disparity Volumes

In many areas of Computer Vision, researchers have found that progressive refinement is a a crucial component for models that require predicting high resolution images [103, 159, 293, 385]. This is often achieved by using skip connections [293] and/or multiple losses at different scales [103, 385]. These methods allow the model to delineate ambiguous results from earlier modules of the network. Following [103], we apply a multi-scale photometric loss (Sec. 3.3.5), and design our network to use progressive refinement. We construct our decoder network to use a DDV layer at a set of different scales $\mathcal{S} = \{\frac{1}{8}, \frac{1}{4}, \frac{1}{2}, \frac{1}{1}\}$ where the scales considered are at $(1/8)$, $(1/4)$, $(1/2)$, and $(1/1)$ of the original image resolution. The disparity maps are then projected using Eq. 3.59 at each scale, as in

$$\sigma(\mathbf{D}^{(s)}(\omega)) = \sum_{k=1}^{K} softmax(\mathbf{D}^{(s)}((i,j))[k]) \times disparity(k), \qquad (3.60)$$

where $\mathbf{D}^{(s)}$ is the disparity volume at a scale $s \in \mathcal{S}$.

Each of the multi-scale decoding layers consists of upconv layers (i.e., nearest upsample + convolution) followed by the DDV layer. To further refine the estimates, the upconv layers also receive skip connections from the ResNet encoder for each of the respective resolution scales. This can be seen in Chapter 6 in Figure 6.2.

3.3.5 Improved Photometric Reprojection Errors

The simplest of photometric reprojection errors is the Mean Absolute Error, used in Section 3.2.5. However, many papers [101,103] have shown that modify[ing] the photometric reprojection loss to incorporate a structural dissimilarity te[rm] (See Section 3.2.9) can improve the estimation results. The dissimilarity te[rm] measures the perceptual dissimilarity between patches in the warped image $\hat{\mathbf{I}}$ a[nd] the original image $\mathbf{I}$. In our model, the photometric error $pe(.)$ is computed [at] each depth scale s by up-sampling the warped image to the original image si[ze]. Mathematically, the improved photometric error is defined as

$$pe(\mathbf{I}_t, \mathbf{I}_{t'}^{(s)}) = \frac{\alpha}{2}(1 - \text{SSIM}(\mathbf{I}_t, \mathbf{I}_{t'}^{(s)})) + (1 - \alpha)\|\mathbf{I}_t - \mathbf{I}_{t'}^{(s)}\|_1, \qquad (3.\blacksquare$$

where α is the weighting term between the mean absolute error and dissimilar[ity] terms.

To encourage disparity estimates to be locally smooth, we follow [101] and ap[ply] an $L1$ penalty on the disparity gradients along both image axes $\partial_x d_t^*$ and $\partial_[y d_t^*]$ where $d_t^* = d_t/\overline{d_t}$ is the mean-normalized inverse depth from [342] which is us[ed] to discourage shrinking of depths estimated by the model. Large depth disco[nti]nuities can often be found in regions with strong image gradients, such as obj[ect] boundaries. To account for this and encourage sharp reconstructions around obj[ect] boundaries, the smoothness term is weighted with an edge aware term using image gradients $\partial \mathbf{I}$. Mathematically, this is formulated as

$$\mathcal{L}_s = |\partial_x d_t^*|e^{-|\partial_x \mathbf{I}|} + |\partial_y d_t^*|e^{-|\partial_y \mathbf{I}|}. \qquad (3.\blacksquare$$

Per-Pixel Minimum Reprojection Loss

In self-supervised depth estimation it is common to compute the photome[tric] reprojection loss over multiple source images and average their contributions. T[his,] however, can cause high photometric error when pixels in the target image $\mathbf{I}_t$ [are] not visible in source image $\mathbf{I}_{t'}$ i.e occluded pixels or out of view pixels at the im[age] borders [103]. Godard *et al.* [103] propose to use a *Minimum Reprojection Loss* wh[ere] the minimum loss is taken over the set of source images, rather than averaging [the] contributions. Following [103], we also apply the *Minimum Reprojection Loss* a[s]

train our models with sequences of 3 temporally adjacent images, including the
target frame $\mathbf{I}_t$ and the source frames $\mathbf{I}_{t'} \in \{\mathbf{I}_{t-1}, \mathbf{I}_{t+1}\}$. Each source frame in $\mathbf{I}_{t'}$ is
warped into the target frame using Eq. 3.54 to forming $\mathbf{I}_{t' \to t}$. Finally the minimum
error is taken between the set of warped source frames, as follows:

$$\mathcal{L}_p = \min_{t'} pe(\mathbf{I}_t, \mathbf{I}_{t' \to t}). \tag{3.63}$$

Automasking of Stationary Pixels

Self-supervised monocular training assumes that the scene under observation
is static and that the camera is moving through the scene. However, in real
world video, these assumptions do not always hold. For example, when there are
moving objects in the scene (i.e other cars) or when the camera is stationary (i.e
at the traffic lights). This results in cases where the depth estimator will exhibit
degenerate behaviour, such as estimating moving objects as 'holes' of infinite
depth. Following [103] we apply 'auto-masking' to filter out pixels that remain
consistent between frames in the sequence. Mathematically, this is computed as

$$\mu^{(s)} = \left[\min_{t'} pe(\mathbf{I}_t, \mathbf{I}_{t' \to t}^{(s)}) < \min_{t'} pe(\mathbf{I}_t, \mathbf{I}_{t'}) \right], \tag{3.64}$$

where $[.]$ represents the Iverson bracket. This results in a binary mask μ which
masks pixels to include values where the re-projection error of $\mathbf{I}_{t' \to t}^{(s)}$ is lower than
the error of the un-warped image $\mathbf{I}_{t'}$, or

$$\mathcal{L}_p = \frac{1}{|\mathcal{S}|} \sum_{s \in \mathcal{S}} \left(\mu^{(s)} \times pe(\mathbf{I}_t, \mathbf{I}_{t' \to t}^{(s)}) \right), \tag{3.65}$$

The masking in (3.65) is calculated and applied for each scale s in the set of possible
resolution scales $\mathcal{S}$. The intuition here is that if the pixel values are similar between
frames in the sequence, this indicates that these pixels correspond to regions that
are static, or regions that are moving with similar relative translation or have low
textural detail.

Final Re-projection Loss

The final loss is computed as the weighted sum of the per-pixel minimum re-
projection loss in (3.61) and smoothness term in (3.62),

$$\mathcal{L} = \mathcal{L}_p + \lambda \mathcal{L}_s, \tag{3.66}$$

where λ weights the smoothness regularisation term. Both the pose model and depth model are trained jointly using this photometric reprojection error. Inference is achieved by taking a test image at the input of the model and producing the high-resolution disparity map $\sigma(\mathbf{D}_{1/1})$, defined in (3.60).

The photometric reprojection loss is a powerful technique for allowing us to train self-supervised depth estimators, using only monocular video sequences as training data. In Chapter 6 we combine the improved photometric reprojection loss (3.61) with the the per-pixel minimum (3.63), auto-masking of stationary pixels (3.64) and edge aware depth smoothness term (3.62) to train a state of the art depth estimation model using self-supervision. To achieve this, our network architecture improves the contextual reasoning of the model by applying the 2D self-attention module (3.57) and produces sharp estimates using the multi-scale discrete disparity volumes (3.60). We show that this architecture significantly outperforms our baseline [103] in the monocular training regime on the KITTI 2015 dataset [95].

CHAPTER **4**

Scaling CNNs for High Resolution Volumetric Reconstruction from a Single Image

The work contained in this chapter has been published as the following paper of which I am the primary author:

Johnston, A., Garg, R., Carneiro, G., Reid, I. and van den Hengel, A., Scaling cnns for high resolution volumetric reconstruction from a single image. In *Proceedings of the IEEE International Conference on Computer Vision Workshops*, pages 939-948, 2017 [155].

Statement of Authorship

Title of Paper	Scaling CNNs for High Resolution Volumetric Reconstruction from a Single Image
Publication Status	☑ Published ☐ Accepted for Publication ☐ Submitted for Publication ☐ Unpublished and Unsubmitted work written in manuscript style
Publication Details	Geometry Meets Deep Learning Workshop (Oral) Proceedings of the IEEE International Conference on Computer Vision Workshops, pages 939-948, 2017

Principal Author

Name of Principal Author (Candidate)	Adrian Johnston
Contribution to the Paper	Ideation, Programming, Experiment Design, Writing, Editing, Presentation.
Overall percentage (%)	80%
Certification:	This paper reports on original research I conducted during the period of my Higher Degree by Research candidature and is not subject to any obligations or contractual agreements with a third party that would constrain its inclusion in this thesis. I am the primary author of this paper.
Signature	Date 08/07/2020

Co-Author Contributions

By signing the Statement of Authorship, each author certifies that:

   i.   the candidate's stated contribution to the publication is accurate (as detailed above);

   ii.   permission is granted for the candidate in include the publication in the thesis; and

   iii.   the sum of all co-author contributions is equal to 100% less the candidate's stated contribution.

Name of Co-Author	Gustavo Carneiro
Contribution to the Paper	Ideation, Experiment Design, Writing, Editing
Signature	Date 08/07/2020

Name of Co-Author	Ravi Garg
Contribution to the Paper	Ideation, Experiment Design, Writing, Editing
Signature	Date 09/07/2020

Name of Co-Author	Ian Reid		
Contribution to the Paper	Ideation and Discussion		
Signature		Date	9/7/2020

Name of Co-Author	Anton van den Hengel		
Contribution to the Paper	Ideation and Discussion		
Signature		Date	9/7/2020

Please cut and paste additional co-author panels here as required.

Abstract

One of the long-standing tasks in computer vision is to use a single 2-D view of an object in order to produce its 3-D shape. Recovering the lost dimension in this process has been the goal of classic shape-from-X methods, but often the assumptions made in those works are quite limiting to be useful for general 3-D objects. This problem has been recently addressed with deep learning methods containing a 2-D (convolution) encoder followed by a 3-D (deconvolution) decoder. These methods have been reasonably successful, but memory and run time constraints impose a strong limitation in terms of the resolution of the reconstructed 3-D shapes. In particular, state-of-the-art methods are able to reconstruct 3-D shapes represented by volumes of at most 32^3 voxels using state-of-the-art desktop computers. In this work, we present a scalable 2-D single view to 3-D volume reconstruction deep learning method, where the 3-D (deconvolution) decoder is replaced by a simple inverse discrete cosine transform (IDCT) decoder. Our simple architecture has an order of magnitude faster inference when reconstructing 3-D volumes compared to the convolution-deconvolutional model, an exponentially smaller memory complexity while training and testing, and a sub-linear runtime training complexity with respect to the output volume size. We show on benchmark datasets that our method can produce high-resolution reconstructions with state of the art accuracy.

4.1   Introduction

Volumetric reconstruction of objects from images has been one of the most studied problems in computer vision [136]. Multi-view reconstruction approaches based on shape by space carving [188] and level-set reconstruction [356] have l to reasonable quality 3-D reconstructions. Systems like KinectFusion [256] a DynamicFusion [255] have opened the possibilities for various applications in field of augmented and virtual reality by providing high quality reconstructi with the help of cheap sensors like Kinect. These multi-view and Kinect bas systems work in constrained environments and disregard scene semantics. It been long believed that a successful estimation of the semantic class, 3-D struct

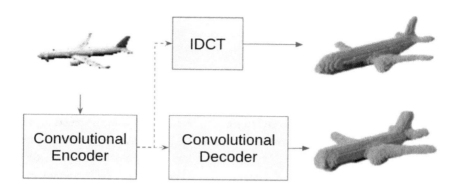

Figure 4.1: We propose a new convolution-deconvolution deep learning model, where the traditional 3-D deconvolutional decoder (bottom) is replaced by an efficient IDCT decoder (top) for high resolution volumetric reconstructions.

and pose of the objects in the scene can be immensely helpful for holistic visual understanding of images [231]. In fact, this estimation would allow intelligent systems to be more effective at interacting with the scene, but one important requirement, particularly regarding the 3-D structure of objects, is to obtain the highest possible 3-D representation resolution at the smallest computational cost – this is precisely the aim of this paper.

Recent success of convolutional neural networks (CNNs) [183, 196] has led to many approaches tackling the challenging problem of volumetric reconstruction from a single image to move towards full 3-D scene understanding [53,291,360,361, 364,370] However, most of these methods reconstructs object at very low resolution ranging from 20^3 to 32^3 voxels – thereby limiting the practical applicability. Almost all these deep networks, designed for single view volumetric reconstructions, rely on a convolution-deconvolution architecture, as shown in Fig. 4.1. In this setup, a traditional 2-D convolution network (often used in classifiers) encodes a large patch of the image into an abstract feature (i.e., an embedded low-dimensional representation), which is then converted into a volume by successive deconvolution operations. These convolution-deconvolution architectures are based on the success of deconvolution networks for semantic segmentation [220, 258] that shows that the loss of resolution due to strided convolutions/pooling operations can be recovered by learning deconvolution filters. These convolution - deconvolution architectures give reasonably accurate reconstructions at low resolution (typically 32^3 voxels or less) from a single image, but do not scale well to high resolution volumetric reconstructions. The main reason behind this issue lies in the successive deconvolution to upscale a coarse reconstruction, which requires intermediate volumetric representations to be learned in succession in a coarse to fine manner, where each deconvolution layer upscales the predictions by a factor of two. Although deconvolution layers have very few parameters, the memory and the time required to process volumes (both for training and inference) in this coarse-to-fine fashion via deconvolution grows rapidly and is intractable. Table 4.1 (see baseline-32 and baseline-128 results) reports how the 3-D resolution affects traditional convolution-deconvolution architectures in terms of memory required for training as well as training and inference running time.

In this work, we explore a simple option in the design of a novel deep learning model that can reconstruct high-resolution 3-D volumes from a single 2-D single view. In particular, our main goal is to have a model that scales well with an increase in resolution of the 3-D volume reconstruction with respect to memory, training time and inference time. One straightforward approach is to learn a linear model (e.g., principal component analysis [156]) or a non-linear model (e.g., Gaussian Process latent variable model [195]) to represent the shapes of the objects and use it in place of the deconvolution network. However, this will make (i) the reconstruction methods sensitive to the 3-D volumetric data used for training, which is not available in abundance and (ii) would not be easily adaptable to semi-supervised methods [265], which does not require 2-D image-volumetric model pairs for training. An alternative solution is the use of the low frequency coefficients computed from the discrete cosine transform (DCT) or Fourier basis which are in general good linear bases to represent smooth signals. In fact, the DCT basis has already been shown to be a robust volume representation [277] as evidenced in Fig. 4.2, which shows that for a representative set of volumetric object shapes taken from ShapeNet [39], the low-frequency DCT basis is much more information preserving then that of the commonly used local interpolation

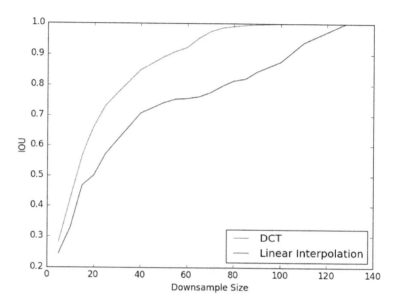

Figure 4.2: Comparison of low frequency 3-D DCT compression accuracy to simple interpolation at various compression rates on a subset of ShapeNet volumes [39]. 128^3 volumes are compressed using (i) nearest neighbour interpolation (blue curve) or (ii) by truncating the high frequency of DCT basis (red curve) and upscaled with respective inverse operations to compute mean IOU.

methods in CNNs for up-sampling low resolution predictions. It is important to note that while being generic, the DCT basis is almost as information preserving as a linear PCA basis when the variability in the dataset increases.

Therefore, we propose a model that extends the convolution-deconvolution network by replacing the computationally expensive deconvolution network by a simple inverse DCT (IDCT) linear transform, as shown in Fig. 4.1, where this IDCT transform reconstructs the low-frequency signal at the desired resolution.

Our proposed extension has profound impact in terms of the computational cost involved in training and inference. In particular, we show through extensive experiments on benchmark datasets that our proposed framework:

- presents an inference time that is one order of magnitude faster than equivalent convolution-deconvolution networks,

- shows a slightly more accurate 3-D object shape prediction than equivalent convolution-deconvolution networks;

- scales gracefully with increase in resolution of the output 3-D volume in terms of training memory requirements, training time, and inference time,

- allows a 3-D volume recovery at a much larger resolution compared to previously proposed approaches in the field.

4.2   Related Work

The problem of reconstructing the 3-D shape of an object from a single image has recently received renewed attention from the field with the use of traditional computer vision methods [336] (e.g., structure-from-motion, optimisation of the visual hull representation, etc.). However, with the advent of deep learning techniques [183] and new datasets containing 3-D model annotations of images containing particular visual objects, the field has moved towards the application of these deep learning models to the task of 3-D reconstruction from images [39,364]. In particular, the seminal paper by Wu *et al.* [364] is the first to propose a deep learning methodology that reconstructs 3-D volumes from depth maps, which has led to several extensions [53,233].

The more recently proposed methods replaced depth maps by the RGB image with the same goal of recovering the 3-D shape of the object from a single or multiple views of it. For instance, Girdhar *et al.* [98] used a 3-stage training process to perform 3-D reconstruction from single images: 1) train a 2-D classifier with mixed synthetic and real images; 2) train a 3-D auto-encoder for learning a representation of their 3-D volumes; and 3) merge the two by minimizing the Euclidean distance between the 2-D and 3-D codes. In parallel, Choy *et al.* [53] developed a recurrent neural network model which aims to use multiple views of a single object to perform 2-D to 3-D reconstruction (the reasoning behind the use of multiple views was to enable the encoding of more information about the object). The use of a projective transformer network that can align the visual object and its projected image allows the unsupervised modelling of 3-D shape reconstruction approaches from single images, as shown by Yan *et al.* [370]. Adversarial training methods for deep learning models [107] have also influenced the development of 3-D shape reconstruction approaches from single images. Wu *et al.* [361] applied a variational encoder and an adversarial decoder for the task of 3-D shape reconstruction from single images. Rezende *et al.* [291] introduced an unsupervised learning framework for recovering 3-D shapes from 2-D projections, with results on the the the recovery of only simple 3-D primitives using reinforcement learning. These methods above are based on a relatively similar underlying convolution-deconvolution network, so they have the same limitations discussed in Sec. 4.1.

State-of-the-art deep learning semantic segmentation models are also based on a similar convolution-deconvolution architectures [97,220,258], so it is useful to understand the functionality of such approaches and assess their applicability for the problem of recovering the 3-D shape of the object from a single view. In particular, these approaches show that fully trainable convolution-deconvolution architectures [258], the exploration of a Laplacian reconstruction pyramid to merge predictions from multiple scales [97], and the use of skip connections [220] can produce state-of-the-art semantic segmentation results. However, it is unclear how to extend these ideas in a computationally efficient manner for the the case of volumetric predictions from images, given the explosion of the number of parameters required to generate volumes at high resolutions.

The high memory, training and inference complexities in processing volumes by an encoder (i.e., the convolutional part of the architecture) has also been addressed in the field [209,292]. Li *et al.* [209] proposed to replace convolutional layers by field probing layers, which is a type of filter that can efficiently extract features from 3-D volumes. However, this method is focused on discriminative

features and is not invertible, so it would not be suitable for 3-D reconstructi
Similarly, a memory and run-time efficient processing of 3-D input data has be
proposed by Riegler *et al.* [292] with a method focused on the classification and s
mentation of volumes and point clouds. That work relies on the use of specializ
convolution, pooling and unpooling layers based on the Octree data structure, a
shows excellent results on scaling up 3-D classification and point cloud segmer
tion. Nevertheless, in order to be applicable for the problem of 3-D reconstructi
from 2-D views, this approach would need to be extended to be able to rece
2-D data as input (instead of 3-D) and output a 3-D representation.

There have been many examples of methods that explore 3-D shape represer
tions, consisting of a relatively small set of principal component analysis (PCA) [
or DCT [64] components that can be further reduced with Gaussian Process Lat
Variable Models (GPLVM) [195]. These methods are successful at several tas
ranging from object shape reconstruction [12,64], image segmentation and tra
ing [277], etc. Finally, Zheng *et al.* [387] show that the use of such low-dimensio
pre-learned representations are useful for the task of object detection from a sin
depth image.

4.3   Methods

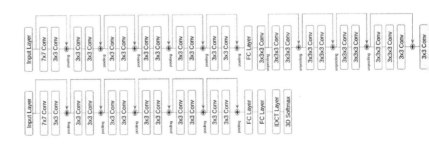

Figure 4.3: Network Architectures: Top: Baseline Network mimicking 3-D R2
[53] without RNN/3-D GRU. Bottom: Our Network utilizing the IDCT Layer

4.3.1   Network Architecture

Our main contribution is in exchanging the decoder with a simple IDCT layer which is compatible with any 2-D encoder architecture. To show the impact of the proposed frequency based representation, we extensively analyze the performance of our IDCT decoder against a deconvolution baseline. We adapt the state-of-the-art convolutional - deconvolution network for volumetric reconstruction called 3-D-R2N2, proposed by Choy *et al.* [53]. The 3-D-R2N2 model [53] iteratively refines reconstructed volumes by using a recurrent module to fuse the 2-D information coming from multiple views, which is then passed to the deconvolution decoder to generate volumetric reconstructions. To restrict the experiments for single-view training and testing, we remove the recurrent module from 3-D-R2N2 and replace it with a single fully connected layer. The result is a simpler convolutional-deconvolutional baseline network, shown in Figure 4.3, as a direct replacement of 3-D-R2N2, for single view reconstruction. In the encoder, we use standard max pooling layers for down sampling, while leaky rectified units are used for the activations with residual connections [123].

Our proposed IDCT decoder uses the same baseline encoder defined above to predict the low frequency DCT coefficients, which our decoder converts to solid volumes. The DCT/IDCT function can be efficiently implemented by utilizing the symmetry and separability properties of the nD-DCT function [285]. That is to say that we can pre-compute the 1D-DCT matrix and apply it independently across each axis of the volume. The Discrete Cosine Function has several variants (e.g DCT-I through DCT-VIII) [285]. In this work we will refer to DCT-II as the DCT function and DCT-III as the IDCT function. The DCT-III function is the inverse of the DCT-II function, furthermore, when the DCT matrix is orthogonal the DCT-III/IDCT is the transpose of the DCT-II matrix [285]. The orthogonal 1D DCT-II is given by:

$$X_k = \left(\frac{2}{N}\right)^{\frac{1}{2}} \sum_{i=0}^{N-1} \Lambda(i) cos\left[\frac{\pi}{N}\left(n+\frac{1}{2}\right)\right] x_i \qquad (4.1)$$

where x_i is the input signal at a given index i, X_k is the output coefficient at index k and Λ is the scaling constant applied to x_0 used to make the transform orthogonal, as defined by

$$\Lambda(i) \begin{cases} \frac{1}{\sqrt{2}} & if\ i = 0 \\ 1 & otherwise \end{cases}. \tag{4.2}$$

In this work, we use the transpose of the DCT-II matrix as our IDCT matrix, however it could also be implemented directly using the DCT-III equation [285]. As our baseline is modeled after 3-D-R2N2, we keep the same loss function defined by the sum of voxel Cross-Entropy [53]:

$$L = \sum_{i,j,k} \{y_{(i,j,k)} \log(p_{(i,j,k)}) + (1 - y_{(i,j,k)}) \log(1 - p_{(i,j,k)})\} \tag{4.3}$$

where $p_{(i,j,k)}$ represents the predicted object occupancy probabilities, $y_{(i,j,k)} \in \{0,1\}$ denotes the given label for voxel (i,j,k)

We use the voxel intersection over union metric [53] to evaluate the quality of our 3-D reconstructions, defined by:

$$IoU = \frac{\sum_{i,j,k} [I(p_{(i,j,k)} > t) I(y_{(i,j,k)})]}{\sum_{i,j,k} [I(p_{(i,j,k)} > t) + I(y_{(i,j,k)})]}, \tag{4.4}$$

where t is the voxelization threshold and $I(.)$ is the indicator function.

4.4 Experiments

Method	Resolution	Batch Size	Forward Time (Hz)	Train time (Hz)	Memory (GB)
DCT-32 - 20^3 coeff	32^3	24	294(4x)	80.75(6.3x)	1.7
Baseline-32	32^3	24	66.83(1x)	12.63(1x)	4.5
DCT-128 - 20^3 coeff	128^3	24	30.48(0.45x)	22.99 (1.8x)	2.2
Baseline-128	128^3	2	2.82 (0.04x)	0.19 (0.015x)	10.4

Table 4.1: Performance indicators using deconvolution and IDCT networks at different resolutions.

To clearly demonstrate the usefulness of our IDCT decoder based volumetric reconstruction method, in this section we first compare the runtime and memory requirement of both deconvolutional and IDCT architectures at two different resolutions of 32^3 and 128^3. To estimate 128^3 volumetric reconstructions with deconvolutional network we simply add two extra deconvolution blocks to the deconvolution baseline of Fig. 4.3.1. An appropriate IDCT basis function is replaced to generate 128^3 volumes from 20^3 coefficients for the proposed method. Table 4.1 shows the training time[1], inference time and the peak GPU memory required to train the baseline and the proposed IDCT based network to reconstruct volumes at both resolutions from 127×127 images[2].

Due to the large reduction in the depth of the our IDCT decoder, our proposed network is approximately four times faster for inference and over six times faster during training, when compared with our baseline model at a smaller resolution of 32^3 with batch size of 24. Furthermore the memory requirements during training are drastically reduced as the intermediate coarser volumes are not predicted by our decoder. When the resolution is increased by a factor of four (in each of the three dimensions), to be 128^3, it becomes evident that the traditional 3-D deconvolution networks become intractable. Already approximately seven times slower and three times more memory hungry deconvolution networks now can only be trained with a batch size of 2 on a 12 GB GPU card. Per-image training goes up by a factor of over 50 compared to 32^3 resolution deconvolution baseline and the test time performance degrades equally drastically making this baseline unusable. Conversely, a single layer IDCT decoder is only three times slower to train when the resolution is increased by a factor of four (in each of the three dimensions) – however it still remains faster to train when compared to the deconvolutional network reconstructing volumes at 32^3 resolution. The memory required for training this IDCT decoder only grows by the size needed to store the high resolution predictions. Training the network for high resolution volumes becomes feasible with a much higher batch size while the number of parameters required remains constant.

To validate the 3-D reconstruction accuracy with the proposed IDCT decoder, we compare the single view reconstruction accuracies on both synthetic (ShapeNet [39]) and real (PascalVOC 3-D+ [366]) datasets. We show that using our single IDCT layer as decoder does not degrade the quality of low-resolution predictions but enables substantially faster training and gives better high resolution reconstructions.

---

[1]Both training and test times are estimated after the data is loaded to the GPUs
[2]Nvidia Titan X (Maxwell), with Intel i7 4970k was used for these experiments.

4.4.1 Experiments on Synthetic Dataset

Following Choy *et. al.* [53], we use synthetically rendered images of resolution
127×127 provided by the authors containing a 13 class subset of the original
ShapeNet [39]. This subset (ShapeNet13) consists of approximately 50,000 2-D-3-D
pairs, with a split of 4/5 for training and 1/5 for testing, exactly as defined in [53].
For all experiments on ShapeNet dataset, we use Theano [325] and Lasagne [69]
libraries for our implementations. In addition, the training procedure uses mini-
batches of size 24 and learning rate of 10^{-5} with Adam [172] optimizer.

We compare the mean IoU error (Table 4.2) of the baseline deconvolution architecture against the proposed IDCT decoder architecture in Table 4.2. As our
baseline can be seen as a simpler version of [53] with one view training, for com-
pleteness, we report results for the entire test-set for our baseline deconvolutional
network alongside that of [53]. As expected, our baseline using only single-view
to predict volumes against five views used in [53] gives marginally lower reconstruction accuracies than that of [53]. However it is important to note that our
IDCT decoder could also be integrated with the RNN as proposed in [53]. For
simplicity, we limit our experiments to the one-view training and testing paradigm.

When compared at 32^3 resolution, our approach with IDCT decoder gives

Method	Resolution	Mean IoU
R2N2 (5V train, 5V test) [53]	32^3	0.634
R2N2 (5V train, 1V test) [53]	32^3	0.6096
Baseline (1V train, 1V test)	32^3	0.5701
DCT - 20^3 coeff	32^3	0.5791
Baseline Upscaled	128^3	0.3988
DCT - 20^3 coeff	128^3	0.4174

Table 4.2: Volumetric shape prediction IoU errors on ShapeNet 3-D.

marginally better volumetric reconstructions (with 20^3 DCT coefficients) com pared to the baseline. However, it is trained in a day and half whereas the baseline takes more than a week to train. A significant boost in accuracy can be seen at 128^3 reconstructions when we fine-tune our network with high resolution ground truth. As shown in Figure 4.4, the reconstructions produced by the baseline approach after upscaling with linear interpolation overestimates the foreground objects, leading to less accurate and blocky reconstructions. On the other hand, our proposed method is able to preserve a significant amount of shape details.

Figure 4.4: Examples of 3-D reconstructions from single view images using the Synthetic ShapeNet13 dataset [39, 53]. First Row: Input Image, Second Row: Ground truth shape, Third Row:32^3 Volumetric prediction using deconvolutional decoder upscaled to 128^3, Bottom Row: Volumetric predictions at 128^3 using the proposed IDCT decoder.

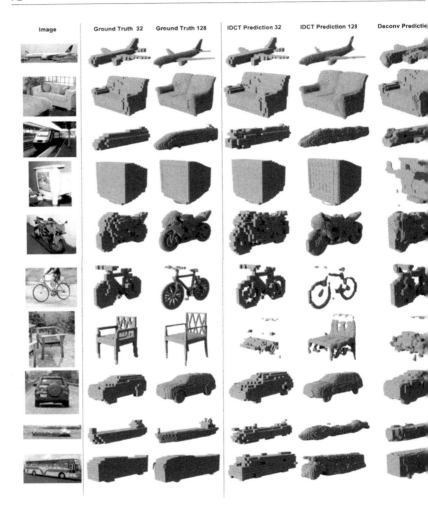

Figure 4.5: Examples of volumetric reconstructions on instances of PASCAL V 3-D+ dataset. From left to right: Input image, ground truth volume at 32^3, grou truth volume at 128^3 resolutions, IDCT decoder based reconstruction at 32^3, IE decoder based reconstruction at 128^3 and the baseline 32^3 reconstruction w deconvolutional decoder upscaled to 128^3 respectively.

4.4.2 Experiment with Real Images

Most of the CNNs based volumetric reconstruction approach [53, 98, 361] use an intermediate step of training the network with a semi-synthetic dataset by augmenting the synthetically rendered object instances with real backgrounds. We choose to directly fine-tune both the deconvolutional and IDCT decoder based networks on real images from PASCAL VOC 3-D+ dataset (specifically we use v1.1 with ImageNet [67] augmentation) [366]. We prune the object instances that are classified as either difficult or truncated, leaving approximately 11400 image instances, which we will use as our training samples. The same pruning strategy is applied to the testing set. Object instances were cropped from the real images to the regions corresponding to 20% dilated bounding boxes for training. Padding with white background was used along the shortest image axis to maintain the aspect ratio when resizing the cropped objects to the input resolution for our network (127x127). Only horizontal flips of images were used for data augmentation while fine tuning.

Our setup of directly fine-tuning the synthetic shapenet model onto PASCAL VOC 3-D+ can be considered to be more challenging compared to other methods due to lack of training data and amount of background clutter and occlusion. These issues make the training more difficult. Following [220], the pre-trained models evaluated in Section 4.4.1 were fine-tuned with a batch size of 1, using stochastic gradient descent (SGD) with higher Nesterov momentum of 0.99 and learning rate of 10^{-5}. Furthermore, in order to reduce over-fitting, we also added dropout to all models as well as weight decay of 10^{-4}.

	Resolution	aero	bike	boat	bus	car	chair	mbike	sofa	train	tv	mean
DCT - 20^3 Coeff	32^3	0.5552	0.4893	0.5231	0.7756	0.6221	0.2497	0.6561	0.4624	0.5739	0.5492	0.5474
Deconvolution Baseline	32^3	0.5492	0.4516	0.5011	0.7593	0.6345	0.244	0.6437	0.546	0.5675	0.5161	0.5419
DCT - 20^3 Coeff	128^3	0.4502	0.2606	0.4067	0.6942	0.561	0.1836	0.5509	0.4311	0.4273	0.5105	0.4496
Baseline upscaled	128^3	0.2824	0.1263	0.336	0.6167	0.5126	0.181	0.4377	0.4654	0.3287	0.4095	0.3671

Table 4.3: Per category and mean volumetric shape prediction IoU errors on PASCAL VOC 3-D+ at 32^3 and 128^3 resolutions.

The IoU errors are compared in Table 4.3 at both 32^3 and 128^3 resolutions. As observed in the synthetic dataset, results for 32^3 resolution with both deconvolution and IDCT decoder methods are similar. Despite the truncation of predictions to 20^3 coefficients, we observe that with the exception of car and sofa, IDCT decoder based reconstruction outperforms the deconvolutional network by narrow margin. More drastic performance gains are observed when high resolution volumes are used for training our IDCT decoder with mean IoU increasing by ~ 22%. Figure 4.5 shows the visual comparison of the results for our proposed IDCT

Figure 4.6: Failure Cases: Truncated and cluttered background throwing off the volumetric reconstructions. From left to right: Input image, ground truth volume at 32^3, ground truth volume at 128^3 resolutions, IDCT decoder based reconstruction at 32^3, IDCT decoder based reconstruction at 128^3 and the baseline 32^3 reconstruction with deconvolutional decoder upscaled to 128^3 respectively.

decoder based network and the deconvolution baseline. We observe that due to the challenging background clutter, occlusion and significant truncation of the training and test instances, both the IDCT and deconvolutional decoder networks are thrown off (see Figure 4.6 for failures). However, for most of the successful reconstruction scenarios, the IDCT decoder based reconstruction were more accurate while preserving details in the object structures evident from images. For example, 3D deconvolutional reconstruction fails to pick up the back of the car and depth of the computer monitor evident in the image to reconstruct the pick-up car or flat-screen whereas proposed method correctly reconstruct the objects. Also note in Figure 4.5 that the 128^3-voxel reconstructions from real images with IDCT often contains much richer details, even though our network was still restricted to estimate 20^3 low frequency DCT coefficients like reconstruction of aeroplane train, motorbike.

As discussed in Tulsiani *et al.* [329], it is important to note that the PASCAL

VOC 3D+ dataset was not originally intended for the purposed of evaluating supervised volumetric reconstruction. The dataset contains a limited number of ground truth CAD models/volumes that are shared in both the training and the test sets. This means that instead of learning to interpolate in the manifold of possible 3D shapes from ShapeNet, neural network with reconstruction loss might over-fit to retrieve the nearest volumetric shape in the training set for every image. An evidence of this can be seen in 128^3 reconstruction of the chair in Figure 4.5 where the style of chair-back is hallucinated or in the reconstruction of sofa which is reconstructed to be a two-seater without evidence in the image. However, in the absence of a better alternative to test on real data and for fair comparison with existing volumetric reconstruction methods, we still use PASCAL VOC 3D+ dataset for evaluation. The aforementioned over-fitting problem can be avoided to some extent by fine tuning on real data in a weakly supervised manner instead of using direct volume supervision with limited CAD models. A perspective projection layer with segmentation loss of projected volumes is used for this purpose in [117, 329, 370, 394]. These weakly supervised modules can be easily deployed with our IDCT decoder to facilitate faster training for high resolution volumetric reconstructions. Finally, thin structures like bike wheels, chair legs are found missing at times in our 128^3-voxel reconstructions, which potentially can be recovered using fully connected CRFs [181] or object connectivity priors [338].

4.5 Conclusions and Future Work

In this paper we have presented a method for reconstructing high resolution 3-D volumes from single view 2-D images, using a decoder based on the inverse Discrete Cosine Transform. Our proposed method is shown to be an order of magnitude faster and require less memory than standard deconvolutional decoders and to be scalable in terms of memory and runtime complexities as a function of the output volume resolution. We also show that it is possible to compress the dimensionality of the prediction with generic DCT basis without losing important details. We observe that a simple dimensionality reduction with a generic basis not only allows for faster inference, but it makes training more stable. For future work, we will study the feasibility of processing both the input images and output volumes in the frequency domain. As most of the training and inference times as well as the memory required for high resolution reconstruction contributes to our loss layer, it will be fruitful to explore robust reconstruction loss in the frequency domain for further speedup.

CHAPTER 5

Single View 3D Point Cloud Reconstruction using Novel View Synthesis and Self-Supervised Depth Estimation

The work contained in this chapter has been published as the following paper:

Johnston, A. and Carneiro, G., Single View 3D Point Cloud Reconstruction using Novel View Synthesis and Self-Supervised Depth Estimation. In *2019 Digital Image Computing: Techniques and Applications (DICTA)* (pp. 1-8). IEEE. 2019 [153].

Statement of Authorship

Title of Paper	Single View 3D Point Cloud Reconstruction using Novel View Synthesis and Self-Supervised Depth Estimation
Publication Status	☑ Published ☐ Accepted for Publication ☐ Submitted for Publication ☐ Unpublished and Unsubmitted work written in manuscript style
Publication Details	Digital Image Computing: Techniques and Applications (DICTA), 2019 (Oral)

Principal Author

Name of Principal Author (Candidate)	Adrian Johnston
Contribution to the Paper	Ideation, Programming, Experiment Design, Writing, Editing, Presentation.
Overall percentage (%)	80%
Certification:	This paper reports on original research I conducted during the period of my Higher Degree by Research candidature and is not subject to any obligations or contractual agreements with a third party that would constrain its inclusion in this thesis. I am the primary author of this paper.
Signature	Date 08/07/2020

Co-Author Contributions

By signing the Statement of Authorship, each author certifies that:

    i.   the candidate's stated contribution to the publication is accurate (as detailed above);

    ii.   permission is granted for the candidate in include the publication in the thesis; and

    iii.   the sum of all co-author contributions is equal to 100% less the candidate's stated contribution.

Name of Co-Author	Gustavo Carneiro
Contribution to the Paper	Writing, Editing
Signature	Date 08/07/2020

Abstract

Capturing large amounts of accurate and diverse 3D data for training is often time consuming and expensive, either requiring many hours of artist time to model each object, or to scan from real world objects using depth sensors or structure from motion techniques. To address this problem, we present a method for reconstructing 3D textured point clouds from single input images without any 3D ground truth training data. We recast the problem of 3D point cloud estimation as that of performing two separate processes, a novel view synthesis and a depth/shape estimation from the novel view images. To train our models we leverage the recent advances in deep generative modelling and self-supervised learning. We show that our method outperforms recent supervised methods, and achieves state of the art results when compared with another recently proposed unsupervised method. Furthermore, we show that our method is capable of recovering textural information which is often missing from many previous approaches that rely on supervision.

5.1 Introduction

Reconstruction of the 3D world from images has been one of the most studied problems in computer vision [323]. Early works which focused on part-based reconstruction using simple geometric shapes [136], multi-view reconstruction using space carving [188], or 3D shape recovery from shading [323], have led to reasonable quality 3-D reconstructions. In more recent years, with the development and standardisation of deep learning [106] in computer vision, researchers and practitioners have focused on applying these techniques to perform single-view [143, 155, 211, 364, 370] and multi-view [52, 329, 370] reconstruction. These methods often employ 3D volumetric representations as they are easily adapted from existing 2D convolutional neural networks (CNN), due to the inherent similarities between 2D images and 3D volumes. Many of the architectures and methods used on 2D images can be "lifted" into 3D by replacing the 2D convolutions with 3D convolutions. However, using volumetric representations in the deep learning framework tend to be limited in terms of quality due to computational inefficiencies. The volumetric representation is information sparse, where 3D shapes are represented by a binary occupancy grid or a signed distance field. This representation contains a substantial amount of redundancy, with most of the information concentrated at the surface voxels. Many follow-up papers have focused on improving 3D CNNs by exploiting the fact that most of the information is concentrated at the surface voxels – this idea has lead to improvements in training time and volumetric resolution [155,292]. Newer papers [78,211] focus on using a point cloud representation, which allow more precise reconstruction with less memory usage. Furthermore, many of the existing systems only try to recover the geometry of the 3D shape, while completely ignoring the textural information.

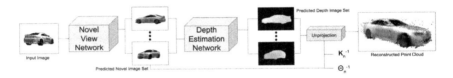

Figure 5.1:   To recover a 3D point cloud from a single image, the Novel View prediction model predicts a set of novel view images at a fixed view points. These novel views are then passed through a Depth Estimation model, where depths are estimated for each of the images in the set. The predicted RGB-D images are then unprojected using the inverse camera intrinsics matrix $\mathbf{K}_n^{-1}$ and the inverse object pose Θ_n^{-1}, for each novel view point n

With the large increase in access to data and improved computational resources, "learning to reconstruct" has become the standard method for single-view 3D reconstruction [52,78,211,364]. However, 3D object data sets are still limited and have varying quality due to being hand modelled by artists. Unlike 2D image data, capturing real world accurate and varied ground truth 3D data is difficult, time consuming and error prone. Our goal is to simultaneously recover both the 3D shape and texture information for a specific object without any 3D supervision. We aim to use only a data set of 2D images to perform our single view 3D reconstruction. This is achieved by using advances in self-supervised depth estimation [94,101] and deep generative modelling [107,280,345]. Our contributions are as follows:

1. We develop a novel framework for single view self-supervised 3D point cloud reconstruction using an image based shape representation;

2. Our method is capable of generating both shape and textural information from a single-view by leveraging advances in deep generative modelling and self-supervised learning; and

3. Our combined novel view synthesis and self-supervised depth estimators are capable of outperforming previous state of the art fully supervised methods on the ShapeNet [39] car dataset.

5.2 Related Work

Deep learning based shape priors [78, 364] take one of the following three shape representations: volumetric, point cloud or polygonal mesh. We will discuss in detail the most relevant methods to our own, which are based on volumetric and point cloud representations. Volumetric shape representation represents a 3D shape as either a binary occupancy grid or as a signed distance field, where grid cell values represent volume occupancy indicators [364] or the distances to the zero level set [323] respectively. Point clouds are made up of a set of 3D coordinates that represent point samples along either the surface of the shape or within the convex hull of the shape. Polygonal meshes, which are typically used in computer graphics, represent a shape with a collection of vertices, edges and faces, where each face consists of triangles or quadrilaterals. When learning shape priors, each of these representations have pros and cons. Volumetric shapes are easy to represent in the deep learning framework as they are analogous in many ways to 2D images, but they are costly in terms of memory usage [155, 292] and training/inference time [155]. Many recent works have focused on trying to improve the efficiency of volumetric representations, through Octrees [292], frequency domain compression via the Discrete Cosine Transform [155] and sparse convolutions [50]. Point cloud representations are easy to work with in the geometric deep learning framework as projections/unprojections and transformations can be implemented with simple matrix multiplications. However, they usually only have a small fixed number of points to represent the shape, meaning that the 3D shapes have limited quality. This is due to the fact that a set of points has to be represented by a fully connected layer [279] or a recurrent neural network [78], where each point is predicted based on previously predicted points in an auto-regressive manner.

5.2.1 Single View 3D Reconstruction

Recovering a 3D shape from a 2D image has been a long-standing goal in the field of computer vision [323]. While many traditional methods, such as structure from motion [323] and multi-view stereo [323] rely on many different views to recover a 3D shape or scene, deep learning based methods aim to "learn to reconstruct" by using large collections of corresponding 2D images and 3D shapes [39]. This is typically done by learning an encoder-decoder model [52], where the encoder is a 2D CNN and the decoder is a 3D deconvolutional neural network. The encoder first produces a representation of the 3D shape, which the decoder then uses to conditionally generate a 3D volume. Using 3D convolutions to recover the shape has many drawbacks. For instance, the volumetric representation limits the reconstructions in terms of shape resolution because of the computational cost of scaling up the representation. Therefore, it is difficult to train models with a high resolution volumetric representation. Furthermore, volumetric representations are inherently sparse – several works have focused on exploiting this fact to improve the performance of volumetric reconstruction methods. Riegler *et al.* [292] redefine the typical 3D convolution and deconvolution operations by a sparse convolution, which uses an Octree to reduce the dimensionality and thereby improve perfor-mance. Johnston *et al.* [155] replace the the 3D deconvolution layers by an inverse discrete cosine transform layer that allows the network to learn the coefficients of the underlying compressed 3D volume, resulting in an order of magnitude improvement in training time, resolution and memory efficiency. To deal with the limited resolution and computation cost of the volumetric representation, Fan *e al.* [78] proposed to instead use a point cloud representation. A deep 2D encode similar to [52], is used to encode the image and a combination of 2D deconvolution and fully connected layers are merged to predict a fixed number of 3D point Another drawback of the naive 3D volumetric representation is the inability to reason about the underlying geometry of the object. Recently, Xinchen *et al.* [370 presented a method that uses a perspective transformation to project the under-lying volume back into a silhouette. They then use a loss function to penalize the projected voxels that are inconsistent with the silhouettes of adjacent views. However, this formulation has difficulty representing concave surfaces as only the visual hull of the object will be projected when computing the loss. To improve upon this method, Tulsiani *et al.* [329] show a method for adding geometric rea-soning, by incorporating a differentiable ray consistency operation, which relaxes the problem and treats the voxel occupancy and projection as a probabilistic grid. This allows the model to handle more complex shapes.

Insafutdinov *et al.* [143] further refine this idea by proposing a CNN that predicts a fixed size point cloud, which is then converted to a probabilistic voxel occupancy grid [329]. Instead of regressing directly for the 3D points, the authors propose to use an unsupervised/self-supervised loss function, where the points are projected back to an image, via a differentiable projection function at random views. This allows the model to use a point cloud re-projection loss to train the network in a self-supervised manner. Furthermore, Insafutdinov *et al.* [143] extend their method by jointly learning an ensemble of pose estimators, such that their method can be trained on images from any pose. However, their model performs significantly worse when relying on such estimated poses for the re-projection loss.

As point clouds are represented as an un-ordered set of 3D points, fully con-nected layers or recurrent neural networks can be used as the output layer for predicting the points [78, 279]. However, in practice, this limits the density of the point cloud as the number of parameters in the output layer increases lin-early with the number of points. Rather than predicting an un-ordered set of points or a 3D volume, Lin *et al.* [211] propose to supervise for depth at a set of given fixed views. Rather than directly regressing for depth, they propose to apply a "pseudo-rendering" function, where the predicted depth maps are first un-projected into a point cloud, then the point cloud is re-projected back into another set of depth maps at random different viewpoints. The supervised loss is then computed against these new depth maps, which forces the model to learn to create a consistent 3D shape. While generating excellent dense point clouds, this method requires the capturing of large amounts of multi-view depth images, which in practice for real data would be prohibitive. Furthermore, this method is unable to recover the underlying 3D texture of the object. Unlike [143], we do not represent our point cloud as a fixed number of points. Instead, we represent our 3D shape using a fixed number of views of an object. We train two separate networks, the first of which predicts N fixed novel views of an object given a single input image. The second network is trained to predict the depth for a given input image. Similarly to [211], we use a depth representation for our 3D shapes. However, we do not supervise for the depth maps, rather we use a photometric image warping loss to train our depth network in a self-supervised manner.

5.2.2 Self-Supervised Depth Estimation

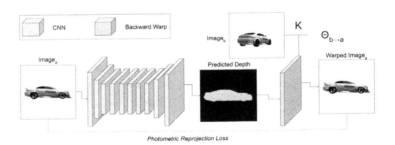

Figure 5.2: The self-supervised depth network is trained using a set of images at different view points with known poses. The input image, $Image_a$ is passed through a CNN which predicts a dense depth map for the image. The predicted depth is then passed into a warping function, along with $Image_b$, the relative pose for the image pair $\theta_{b \rightarrow a}$ and the camera intrinsics matrix $\mathbf{K}$. The warping function uses a differentiable image sampler [147] to re-project the $Image_b$ into the pose of $Image_a$. Finally, the network is trained using a photometric consistency loss function (eq. 5.1), which allows the network to implicitly learn to predict depth, without any ground truth depth images.

In the standard supervised setting, a convolutional neural network is used to estimate depth by supervising against ground truth depth maps captured from any form of depth sensor e.g. Microsoft Kinect, Stereo Depth Maps, LIDAR

However, each of these sensors have limitations with regards to range and operating compatibility (e.g. weather or lighting conditions). Furthermore, ground truth RGB-D data is still limited in variety and size when compared with RGB image data sets. Recent works have shown that it is possible to self-supervise neural networks such that they can implicitly solve the task of interest. This is achieved by using a proxy loss function that solves a closely related problem. This allows networks to be trained from scratch on large collections of unlabelled data. In the case of self-supervised depth models, a photometric error based on differentiable image warping [147] and re-projection is used to implicitly train the network to predict depth. Garg *et al.* [94] show the earliest example of self-supervised depth estimation, performed by using synchronized stereo pairs. These results were further improved by Godard *et al.* [101] with the addition of a left-right consistency term. The photometric loss is extended to compute the loss bidirectionally from left to right and right to left for both images in the pair, ensuring consistency between the depths. Further work in this area has relaxed the requirement of needing stereo pairs, by using monocular video. More specifically, instead of using the stereo information for self-supervision, a second neural network simultaneously predicts the camera pose between frames in the input video [102,339] and image warping is performed between successive frames. As these methods rely on predicted pose values, they are typically worse than the stereo based methods [94,102,339].

5.2.3 Novel View Synthesis

Novel view synthesis is an image based rendering technique, where instead of using a traditional graphics engine, like those found in many 3D applications (e.g. video games, architectural visualization), a model is used to approximate the rendering function. In recent works, an encoder-decoder CNN is used to approximate the rendering function [267,390]. Alternatively, Zhou *et al.* [390] formulate the problem as that of regressing the 2D optical flow field that transforms the input image into the selected target image. In *Transformation Grounded Image Generation Network for Novel 3D View Synthesis* (TVSN) [267], this idea is extended to also include a term to predict the visibility of each pixel. Using this visibility map they mask the occluded pixels and then fill in the missing information using a refinement network. This is combined with an adversarial loss [107] and a perceptual feature matching loss [152], which is used to improve training stability [267, 345]. However, TVSN requires that the visibility maps be computed ahead of time when rendering the objects. This limits the technique to only work on synthetic data sets where it is possible to compute accurate 3D visibility maps ahead of time.

5.3 Methods

Our goal is to generate the 3D textured point cloud of a single object given a single input view. Our training set consists of a set of multi-view observations for several instances of objects from the same category, together with their respective pose. We propose to replace the supervised point cloud estimation, by using a set of depth maps automatically predicted from novel views generated by a deep generative model. Rather than supervising for depth prediction [211], we leverage the advances in self-supervised/unsupervised depth estimation [94, 101]. These depths can then be un-projected to recover a partial point cloud for each generated novel view image. As the model predicts the novel fixed views, we can estimate the depth, un-project using the known camera intrinsics and then combine the N partial point clouds into a single 3D point cloud using the inverse of the object pose. In our experiments, we set the number of camera poses to $N = 5$ at fixed 60 degree intervals, such that they have overlapping fields of view. We exclude the final image (i.e 360°) as it is identical to the first image in the sequence. These output viewpoints are independent from the object pose in the input image.

5.3.1 Self-Supervised Depth Estimation

To estimate the 3D point cloud for a set of images, we train a self-supervised monocular depth estimator. First, a convolutional neural network is used predict the depth for a given input image $I_a : \Omega \to \mathbb{R}^3$, where Ω denotes image lattice. Then, using the vectorized homogeneous depth points[1] $Z_a \in \mathbb{R}^{N \times 4}$ (4th dimension represents the homogeneous coordinate), known camera intrinsics $K \in \mathbb{R}^{4 \times 4}$ and

---

[1]The x and y coordinates are uniformly sampled from a 2D grid between $[-1, 1]$ for each spatial location in I_a.

relative camera pose $\mathbf{T}_{b \to a} \in \mathbb{R}^{4 \times 4}$, the next image in the set $\mathbf{I}_b$ is un-projected and transformed into a matrix of homogeneous points $\mathbf{P}_b \in \mathbb{R}^{N \times 4}$. The un-projected points are transformed back into the source target frame and then re-projected. This process is defined as follows:

$$\mathbf{P}_b = \mathbf{KT}^{-1}(\mathbf{K}^{-1}\mathbf{Z}_a^T). \tag{5.1}$$

The point set $\mathbf{P}_b$ in (5.1) is then sampled using a differentiable image sampler [147], such that the pixels in the source image are warped into the original image

$$\hat{\mathbf{I}}_a = \phi(\mathbf{I}_b, \mathbf{P}_b), \tag{5.2}$$

where $\phi(.)$ denotes the differential sampler defined by [147].

The photometric re-projection error [94, 101] is then computed between the warped image and the original input image. This forces the model to implicitly learn to predict depth for the input image. At test time, only a single image is needed to predict the depth output. The photometric re-projection loss function is computed for each pixel coordinate (x, y) as follows:

$$\mathcal{L}_{pe} = \sum_{x,y} \|\mathbf{I}_a(x, y) - \hat{\mathbf{I}}_a(x, y)\|_1. \tag{5.3}$$

The photometric re-projection loss can be any image reconstruction loss function computed in pixel space. In our case, we find that using a mean absolute error (i.e., L1 distance) is sufficient and provides sharper depth estimates than L2 distance. An overview of this process can be found in Fig. 5.2

5.3.2   Novel View Synthesis

While it is possible to only use a novel view synthesis model with a simple regression loss, this often leads to blurry and inaccurate images (see Table 5.2 for a comparison). As our method requires chaining together image synthesis and a depth estimation, we aim to generate accurate novel views such that the point cloud can be as accurate as possible. Therefore, to improve the image quality we train our novel view model as a generative adversarial network [107] (GAN). The object of the GAN framework is to train two networks, the generator network $G(.)$ which attempts to generate samples that are real enough to fool the discriminator network $D(.)$. These networks are then trained in an alternating fashion[2]. Empirically, we find that the standard adversarial loss [107] is unstable and fails to give satisfactory results. Therefore, we opt to use the least squares generative adversarial loss (LSGAN) [230] formulation, which shows more stable results during training. The LSGAN loss functions for the discriminator network $D(.)$ is defined by:

$$\mathcal{L}_{dis}(G, D) = \frac{1}{2}\mathbb{E}[(D(I_y) - 1)^2] + \frac{1}{2}\mathbb{E}[(D(G(I_x)))^2], \tag{5.4}$$

where I_x is the input image and I_y is the ground truth images for each of the novel viewpoints associated with I_x. The loss function for the generator network $G(.)$ is defined as:

$$\mathcal{L}_{gan}(G, D) = \mathbb{E}[(D(G(I_x)) - 1)^2]. \tag{5.5}$$

We wish to generate the highest possible resolution point cloud, we therefore need to synthesize high resolution novel views. As GANs often struggle with generating images with a resolution greater than 128x128, Iizuka *et al.* [141] and Wang *et al.* [345] suggest that using multiple discriminators at different image scales improves with both the local and global consistency of synthesized images at high resolution. Each discriminator is trained at a different scale improving training stability. Similarly to Wang *et al.* [345], we use three scales, represented by $k \in \{1, 2, 3\}$, and optimizing the generator adversarial loss (5.5) as the sum of the multiple scale discriminator outputs:

$$\min_{G} \max_{D1, D2, D3} \sum_{k=1,2,3} \mathcal{L}_{gan}(G, D_k), \tag{5.6}$$

where D_k represents the Discriminator network for each scale k. We also use an adversarial feature matching loss [267, 345] to improve training stability. The feature matching loss extracts multiple feature maps from the different scale intermediate layers of the Discriminator network. The $L1$ error is then computed between the feature representations for both the real images samples and the synthesized images. This feature matching loss is computed for each of the

---

[2]This process can be thought of as a zero-sum game where the objective is to find a Nash Equilibrium between the two networks.

multiple scale discriminators D_k, as follows:

$$\mathcal{L}_{feat}(G, D_k) = \sum_{i=0}^{T} \frac{1}{N_i} \|D_k^{(i)}(I_y) - D_k^{(i)}(G(I_x))\|_1, \quad (5.7)$$

where T represents the number of intermediate layers. The error between the feature maps is then weighted by the size of each feature map N_i at each intermediate feature scale i. As we are training a conditional GAN we also use a reconstruction term to encourage the network to create exact reconstructions:

$$\mathcal{L}_{recon}(G) = \|I_y - G(I_x)\|_1. \quad (5.8)$$

where the reconstruction loss (5.8) is computed between the synthesised images $G(I_x)$ and the corresponding ground truth images I_y. The final loss function for training the refinement/novel-view network is then computed as the weighted sum of the previous equations:

$$\min_G \mathcal{L}(G, D) = \mathcal{L}_{recon} * \lambda_1 + \mathcal{L}_{feat} * \lambda_2 + \mathcal{L}_{gan} * \lambda_3. \quad (5.9)$$

As the $G(.)$ and $D(.)$ networks are trained in an alternating fashion, the final objective for training the multi-scale discriminator networks is to minimize the sum of the discriminative loss in (5.4) for each of the different scales k:

$$\min_{D1, D2, D3} \sum_{k=1,2,3} \mathcal{L}_{dis}(G, D_k). \quad (5.10)$$

5.3.3 Unprojection and Masking

Finally, it is possible to estimate the 3D point cloud for a set of novel images generated by the novel view network, by passing the novel views through the trained depth estimator. These depths can then be un-projected to form the final point cloud $P \in \mathbb{R}^{N \times 4}$ by performing (5.11) but stopping before re-projection. Given the vectorized depth points $\mathbf{Z}_n \in \mathbb{R}^{N \times 4}$ for each of the novel view points n, known camera intrinsics $\mathbf{K} \in \mathbb{R}^{4 \times 4}$ and relative camera poses $\mathbf{T}_n \in \mathbb{R}^{4 \times 4}$ we can un-project the point cloud for each viewpoint by:

$$P = \mathbf{T_n^{-1}}(\mathbf{K}^{-1}\mathbf{Z}_n^T) \quad \forall n, \quad (5.11)$$

where n denotes the index of the novel view. As the self-supervised depth estimation model is trained implicitly via the image warping function, the model will still attempt to estimate depth for undefined regions. If we were using real images it would be possible to remove background and outlying points based solely on the depth value. However, as the rendered images from ShapeNet data set have no background, we decide to predict the object mask along side the RGB channels in the novel view synthesis. When performing the un-projection, we can mask the background depth image values using this predicted mask.

5.4 Experiments

We evaluate the efficacy of our system for single view 3D point cloud reconstruction using the *car* category of the ShapeNet data set [39]. The images in this data set are taken at uniformly sampled poses and have 256×256 pixels. We select the car class due to its large number of varied instances with high textural detail. We use an instance-wise split of 80%/20% for training and testing, exactly as defined in [52,78,143,155,211]. A UNet network [293] is used for both the depth prediction network and the novel view network. Both networks use convolutional encoder blocks consisting of a strided convolution, batch normalization [106] and leaky ReLU [106]. The convolutional decoder differs between the two architectures. The depth prediction network uses UpConv blocks (bilinear upsample + convolution) as we found that using a transposed convolution results in unacceptable artifacts. In the novel view network, we found that the transposed convolution layers were necessary to stabilize the GAN training [280]. All up-sampling blocks make use of batch normalization and leaky ReLU. We train our novel view network and discriminator using the Adam optimizer with learning rate 0.0002 and 0.0004 respectively. Furthermore, we set the hyper-parameters that control the momentum in the Adam optimizer to $\beta_1 = 0.0$ and $\beta_2 = 0.999$ for both $G(.)$ and $D(.)$. We set the loss function weights (Eq. 5.9) as $\lambda_1 = 100$, $\lambda_2 = 1$ and $\lambda_3 = 1$. To train the depth estimator, we use the Adam optimizer with learning rate 0.001 with default momentum. For each batch, the input/target $\mathbf{I}_a$ view and source view point $\mathbf{I}_b$ randomly selected from the data set to be corresponding views that are rotated $20°$ from one another. Training hyperparameters were selected via manual search.

5.4.1 Evaluation Metrics

Shape Metric

To quantitatively evaluate our 3D point clouds, we opt to use the Chamfer distance metric [78, 211] as it has been shown to be highly correlated with human judgment of 3D shape similarity. Given a ground truth point cloud $\mathbf{P}_{gt}$ and a predicted point cloud $\mathbf{P}_{pr}$, the distance is defined as follows:

$$d_{Chamf}\left(\mathbf{P}_{gt}, \mathbf{P}_{pr}\right) = \min \left\|\mathbf{P}_{pr} - \mathbf{P}_{gt}\right\|_2 + \min \left\|\mathbf{P}_{gt} - \mathbf{P}_{pr}\right\|_2 \tag{5.12}$$

The Chamfer distance is defined by a sum of two components. The left-hand component measures the precision, or how similar the predicted point cloud is to the ground truth. While the right-hand side is the coverage of the predicted point cloud, which measures how well the points cover the surface of the object.

Image Metric

To measure the image generation quality we use the structured similarity image metric (SSIM) [350] The SSIM metric is often used as a perceptual measure of the quality of an image and has been show to have a strong correlation with human perception of image quality [350]. The SSIM measure is computed between the two sets of image patches of size $W \times W$ extracted from the predicted image $\hat{x}$ and ground truth image x:

$$SSIM(\hat{x}, x) = \frac{(2\mu_{\hat{x}}2\mu_x + c_1)(2\sigma_{\hat{x}x} + c_2)}{(\mu_{\hat{x}}^2 + \mu_x^2 + c_1)(\sigma_{\hat{x}}^2 + \sigma_x^2 + c_2)}, \tag{5.13}$$

where $\mu_{\hat{x}}$ and μ_x are the means for each window, and $\sigma_{\hat{x}}$ and σ_x are the variance for each window. While $\sigma_{\hat{x}x}$ is the covariance between the windows $\hat{x}$ and x, the constants are set to the default values of $c_1 = 0.01^2$ and $c_2 = 0.03^2$, and the window size is set to the default value of $W = 11$. The measure returns a value in the range $[0.0, 1.0]$ with 1.0 being perfect recreation of the original image.

5.4.2 Single-view Reconstruction

The quantitative results for the single view object reconstruction task are reported in Table 5.1. When comparing the Chamfer distance (5.12) of our system with several supervised methods [52,78,211], we observe that we outperform all other reported methods. We likely outperform the simpler point cloud and volumetric methods [52,78] due to the denser representation afforded by using a depth map representation. Note that as 3D-R2N2 [52] uses a 3D volumetric representation, the shapes are converted to a point cloud via uniform sampling along the boundary of the volume, severely limiting the final resolution of the point cloud representation. Furthermore, we outperform the method in [211], which also uses a depth map based representation, however, unlike us their method is supervised for depth and is unable to recover textural information. We argue that the improvement over the supervised depth estimator [211] is due to the use of the geometric loss function to train the depth network. While our model under-performs in terms of coverage metric in (5.12), when compared with Lin *et al.* [211], we believe this is due to the simplifying setup that we rely on, consisting of novel views images with zero-degree elevation. As the images have zero elevation, points that are partially self-occluded (e.g. on the bonnet or roof of the car) will be sparser than points in direct view. In future, this could be addressed by using multiple elevations in the novel view network. We also compare with the current state of the art method [143], which also uses self-supervised learning to estimate the 3D point cloud. Our method slightly outperforms with respect to Chamfer distance, but the exact numbers for the method in [143] regarding precision and coverage are unavailable for a more detailed analysis. It is clear from the qualitative results shown in Fig. 5.3, that our method fails to preserve high frequency information like racing stripes or decals, even when utilizing a GAN. However, the general shape and colour are consistent, with some fine details being recovered.

5.4.3   Ablation Study

As our novel view network has a complex training process, we also performed an ablation study to show the efficacy of the GAN method and the proposed architecture. The results presented in Table 5.2 use the same training setup as used in Section 5.4.2. We evaluate the use of a simple Encoder-Decoder model which contains no skip connections, but otherwise is architecturally the same as the UNet. We also show results without the GAN loss function, trained only with $L1$ loss for the Encoder-Decoder model. Furthermore, we also evaluate the us

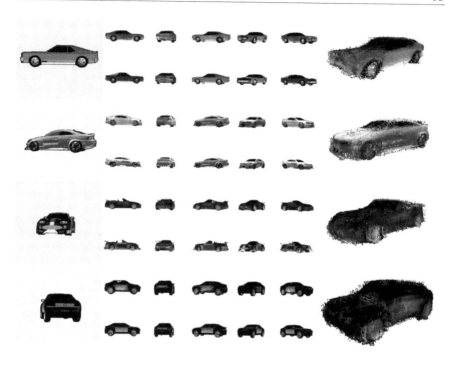

Figure 5.3: **Qualitative results** for the cars category on the ShapeNet test set. Our method is capable of synthesizing coherent and accurate 3D point clouds, with textural (colour) information, using only a single image as input. *Left:* Input image, *Middle-Top:* predicted novel views, *Middle-Bottom:* ground truth test images, *Right:* 3D point clouds, un-projected using the depth and novel view networks.

of the Multi-Scale and Discriminator Feature Matching losses in (5.8) for both the Encoder-Decoder model and the UNet model. Finally, we also tested our novel view model using a Variational Autoencoder (VAE) [106], another type of deep generative model. We also present the results for the UNet without the multi-scale and feature matching discriminators [267, 345]. The comparison is based on the SSIM result over the test set for each of the different methods – see Table 5.2. It is clear from the results that each of the architectural and extra losses, such as

Method	Car
3D-R2N2 (1 view) [52]	1.808 / 3.238 / 5.046
3D-R2N2 (3 view) [52]	1.685 / 3.151 / 4.836
3D-R2N2 (5 view) [52]	1.664 / 3.146 / 4.810
Fan *et al.* [78]	1.800 / 2.053 / 3.853
Lin *et al.* [211]	1.446 / **1.061** / 2.507
Insafutdinov and Dosovitskiy [143]	- / - / 2.42
Proposed (1 view)	**1.208** / 1.208 / **2.416**

Table 5.1: Quantitative results of our method in single view 3D reconstruction compared against several supervised (above line) and self-supervised (below line) systems. Numbers reported are point cloud precision/coverage/Chamfer distance (5.12). The best numbers for each category are in bold font (lower is better).

Method	SSIM	Chamfer
Deep Convolutional VAE	0.8410	2.623
Encoder-Decoder (No GAN)	0.8475	2.692
Encoder-Decoder (GAN)	0.8493	2.476
Encoder-Decoder (GAN + MS + FM)	0.8550	2.43
UNet (GAN + MS + FM)	**0.8756**	**2.416**

Table 5.2: Ablation study results of the ShapeNet Car category. Image quality results are evaluated using the structured similarity metric in (5.13) (higher is better) and the Point Cloud Chamfer distance (5.12) (lower is better). MS: Multi-scale Discriminator. FM: Discriminator Feature Matching Loss. The best numbers for each category are in bold font.

multi-scale and feature matching discriminators, are required to achieve a state of the art result with our method. Counter-intuitively, we found that the skip connections provide a significant improvement in SSIM, Chamfer distance and overall 3D reconstruction quality. Normally, skip connections are used to pass high level structural details for observable details in the input image e.g. object edges and boundaries. Therefore, there should be limited improvement by adding in skip connections, as there will be limited overlap between observable feature and predicted novel views. We believe there are two reasons for the improvement when using skip connections. The first is that the encoder-decoder cannot easily recover the finer details of the texture as there is limited capacity in the hidden layer for representing the 256 × 256-pixel images. Furthermore, it is challenging for the encoder-decoder to correctly estimate the overall colour of an object resulting in blurry and patchy texturing, as can be seen in Fig. 5.4. Secondly, we empirically found that the UNet model is more stable when training the GAN. We believe this is because when one of the target views and the input view are very similar, the network has an easier task of predicting that novel view as it can simply "copy" many of the pixels to the output. The result of this is that the discriminator cannot overpower the generator network as easily. Furthermore, as objects like cars have many textural symmetries, the skip connections can provide important cues to the model about the shape and symmetries of the objects we are trying to reconstruct.

Figure 5.4: Comparison of our method without using UNet skip connections (left) and when using skip connections (right).

5.5 Conclusions and Future Work

In this work, we have presented a method for reconstructing textured 3D point clouds from single images. We achieved this result by leveraging the advances in both deep generative modelling and self-supervised depth estimation. We have shown state of the art results for 3D point cloud reconstruction for the car category in the ShapeNet data set [39]. Future work will focus on extending this method to work for multiple categories, by making use of new improvements in deep generative modelling [161]. To allow for training on images with limited textural detail (Chairs and Airplanes), our method could be further improved by unifying the depth and novel view networks with the incorporation of a differentiable projection function, similar to that presented in [143]. The depth network could be further improved by using both multi-scale [339] and structural dissimilarity loss functions [102] and the Novel View model could be extended to include both geometric reasoning and refinement [267]. Additionally, our method assumes known ground truth poses for performing the reconstruction. By incorporating a 3D pose estimator [102, 339], it would be possible to remove this limitation and train a fully unsupervised 3D reconstruction model.

CHAPTER **6**

Self-supervised Monocular Trained Depth Estimation using Self-attention and Discrete Disparity Volume

The work contained in this chapter has been published as the following paper of which I am the primary author:

Johnston, A. and Carneiro, G., Self-supervised Monocular Trained Depth Estimation using Self-attention and Discrete Disparity Volume. In *Proceedings of the IEEE/CVF Conference on Computer Vision and Pattern Recognition*, pages 4756-4765. 2020. [154]

Statement of Authorship

Title of Paper	Self-supervised Monocular Trained Depth Estimation using Self-attention and Discrete Disparity Volume
Publication Status	☑ Published ☐ Accepted for Publication ☐ Submitted for Publication ☐ Unpublished and Unsubmitted work written in manuscript style
Publication Details	CVPR 2020 Proceedings of the IEEE/CVF Conference on Computer Vision and Pattern Recognition, pages 4756-4765. 2020 (Poster)

Principal Author

Name of Principal Author (Candidate)	Adrian Johnston
Contribution to the Paper	Ideation, Programming, Experiment Design, Writing, Editing, Presentation.
Overall percentage (%)	80%
Certification:	This paper reports on original research I conducted during the period of my Higher Degree by Research candidature and is not subject to any obligations or contractual agreements with a third party that would constrain its inclusion in this thesis. I am the primary author of this paper.
Signature	Date 08/07/2020

Co-Author Contributions

By signing the Statement of Authorship, each author certifies that:

    i.   the candidate's stated contribution to the publication is accurate (as detailed above);

    ii.   permission is granted for the candidate in include the publication in the thesis; and

    iii.   the sum of all co-author contributions is equal to 100% less the candidate's stated contribution.

Name of Co-Author	Gustavo Carneiro
Contribution to the Paper	Writing, Editing
Signature	Date **08/07/2020**

Abstract

Monocular depth estimation has become one of the most studied applications in computer vision, where the most accurate approaches are based on fully supervised learning models. However, the acquisition of accurate and large ground truth data sets to model these fully supervised methods is a major challenge for the further development of the area. Self-supervised methods trained with monocular videos constitute one the most promising approaches to mitigate the challenge mentioned above due to the wide-spread availability of training data. Consequently, they have been intensively studied, where the main ideas explored consist of different types of model architectures, loss functions, and occlusion masks to address non-rigid motion. In this paper, we propose two new ideas to improve self-supervised monocular trained depth estimation: 1) self-attention, and 2) discrete disparity prediction. Compared with the usual localised convolution operation, self-attention can explore a more general contextual information that allows the inference of similar disparity values at non-contiguous regions of the image. Discrete disparity prediction has been shown by fully supervised methods to provide a more robust and sharper depth estimation than the more common continuous disparity prediction, besides enabling the estimation of depth uncertainty. We show that the extension of the state-of-the-art self-supervised monocular trained depth estimator Monodepth2 with these two ideas allows us to design a model that produces the best results in the field in KITTI 2015 and Make3D, closing the gap with respect self-supervised stereo training and fully supervised approaches.

6.1 Introduction

Perception of the 3D world is one of the main tasks in computer/robotic vision. Accurate perception, localisation, mapping and planning capabilities are predicated on having access to correct depth information. Range finding sensors such as LiDAR or stereo/multi-camera rigs are often deployed to estimate depth for use in robotics and autonomous systems, due to their accuracy and robustness. However, in many cases it might be unfeasible to have, or rely solely on such expensive or complex sensors. This has led to the development of learning-based methods [162, 303, 304], where the most successful approaches rely on fully super vised convolutional neural networks (CNNs) [73,74,88,113,234]. While supervised learning methods have produced outstanding monocular depth estimation results ground truth RGB-D data is still limited in variety and abundance when compared with the RGB image and video data sets available in the field. Furthermore, col lecting accurate and large ground truth data sets is a difficult task due to senso noise and limited operating capabilities (due to weather conditions, lighting, etc.

Recent studies have shown that it is instead possible to train a depth estimato in a self-supervised manner using synchronised stereo image pairs [94, 101] o monocular video [388]. While monocular video offers an attractive alternativ to stereo based learning due to wide-spread availability of training sequences, i poses many challenges. Unlike stereo based methods, which have a known camer pose that can be computed offline, self-supervised monocular trained depth est mators need to jointly estimate depth and ego-motion to minimise the photometri reprojection loss function [94, 101]. Any noise introduced by the pose estimato model can degrade the performance of a model trained on monocular sequence resulting in large depth estimation errors. Furthermore, self-supervised monocula training makes the assumption of a moving camera in a static (i.e., rigid) scen which causes monocular models to estimate 'holes' for pixels associated wit moving visual objects, such as cars and people (i.e., non-rigid motion). To dea with these issues, many works focus on the development of new specialised arch tectures [388], masking strategies [103, 225, 339, 388], and loss functions [101,103 Even with all of these developments, self-supervised monocular trained dept estimators are less accurate than their stereo trained counterparts and significantl less accurate than fully supervised methods.

In this paper, we propose two new ideas to improve self-supervised monocu lar trained depth estimation: 1) self-attention [335, 347], and 2) discrete disparit volume [168]. Our proposed self-attention module explores non-contiguous (i.e global) image regions as a context for estimating similar depth at those region Such approach contrasts with the currently used local 2D and 3D convolutions tha

Figure 6.1: **Self-supervised Monocular Trained Depth Estimation using Self-attention and Discrete Disparity Volume**. Our self-supervised monocular trained model uses self-attention to improve contextual reasoning and discrete disparity estimation to produce accurate and sharp depth predictions and depth uncertainties. *Top: input image; Middle Top: estimated disparity; Middle Bottom: samples of the attention maps produced by our system (blue indicates common attention regions); Bottom: pixel-wise depth uncertainty (blue: low uncertainty; green/red: high/highest uncertainty).*

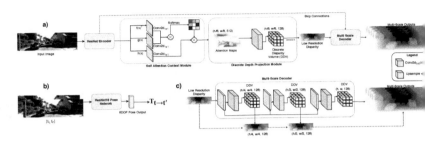

Figure 6.2: **Overall Architecture** The image encoding processes is highlighted
part *a)*. The input monocular image is encoded using a ResNet encoder and th
passed through the Self-Attention Context Module. The computed attention ma
are then convolved with a 2D convolution with the number of output chann
equal to the number dimensions for the Discrete Disparity Volume (DDV). T
DDV is then projected into a 2D depth map by performing a *softargmax* across
disparity dimension resulting in the lowest resolution disparity estimation (Eq. (
In part *b)* the pose estimator is shown, and part *c)* shows more details of the M
Scale decoder. The low resolution disparity map is passed through success
blocks of UpConv (nearest upsample + convolution). The DDV projection
performed at each scale, in the same way as in the initial encoding stage. Fin
each of the outputs are upsampled to input resolution to compute the photome
reprojection loss.

are unable to explore such global context. The proposed discrete disparity volu
enables the estimation of more robust and sharper depth estimates, as previou
demonstrated by fully supervised depth estimation approaches [168, 213]. Shar
depth estimates are important to improving accuracy, and increased robustnes
desirable to allow self-supervised monocular trained depth estimation to add
common mistakes made by the method, such as incorrect pose estimation a
matching failures because of uniform textural details. We also show that
method can estimate pixel-wise depth uncertainties with the proposed disc
disparity volume [168]. Depth uncertainty estimation is important for refin
depth estimation [88], and in safety critical systems [166], allowing an agen

identify unknowns in an environment in order to reach optimal decisions. As a secondary contribution of this paper, we leverage recent advances in semantic segmentation network architectures that allow us to train larger models on a single GPU machine. Experimental results show that our novel approach produces the best self-supervised monocular depth estimation results for KITTI 2015 and Make3D. We also show in the experiments that our method is able to close the gap with self-supervised stereo trained and fully supervised depth estimators.

6.2 Related Work

Many computer vision and robotic systems that are used in navigation, localization and mapping rely on accurately understanding the 3D world around them [4,71, 116,238]. Active sensors such as LiDAR, Time of Flight cameras, or Stereo/Multi camera rigs are often deployed in robotic and autonomous systems to estimate the depth of an image for understanding the agent's environment [4,71]. Despite their wipe-spread adoption [296], these systems have several drawbacks [71], including limited range, sensor noise, power consumption and cost. Instead of relying on these active sensor systems, recent advances leveraging fully supervised deep learning methods [73,74,88,113,234] have made it possible to learn to predict depth from monocular RGB cameras [73,74]. However, ground truth RGB-D data for supervised learning can be difficult to obtain, especially for every possible environment we wish our robotic agents to operate. To alleviate this requirement, many recent works have focused on developing self-supervised techniques to train monocular depth estimators using synchronised stereo image pairs [94,101,273], monocular video [103,388] or binocular video [103,225,379].

6.2.1 Monocular Depth Estimation

Depth estimation from a monocular image is an inherently ill-posed problem as pixels in the image can have multiple plausible depths. Nevertheless, methods based on supervised learning have been shown to mitigate this challenge and correctly estimate depth from colour input images [304]. Eigen *et al.* [74] proposed the first method based on Deep Learning, which applies a multi-scale convolution neural network and a scale-invariant loss function to model local and global features within an image. Since then, fully supervised deep learning based methods have been continuously improved [88, 113, 234]. However these methods are limited by the availability of training data, which can be costly to obtain. While such issues can be mitigated with the use of synthetic training data [234], simulated environments need to be modelled by human artists, limiting the amount of variation in the data set.

To overcome fully supervised training set constraint, Garg *et al.* [94] propose a self-supervised framework, where instead of supervising using ground truth depth, a stereo photometric reprojection warping loss is used to implicitly learn depth. This loss function is a pixel-based reconstruction loss that uses stereo pairs where the right image of the pair is warped into the left using a differentiable image sampler [148]. This loss function allows the deep learning model to implicitly recover the underlying depth for the input image. Expanding on this method Godard *et al.* [101] add a left-right consistency loss term which helps to ensure consistency between the predicted depths from the left and right images of the stereo pair. While capable of training monocular depth estimators, these methods still rely on stereo-based training data which can still be difficult to acquire. This has motivated the development of self-supervised monocular trained depth estimators [388] which relax the requirement of synchronized stereo image pairs by jointly learning to predict depth and ego-motion with two separate networks enabling the training of a monocular depth estimator using monocular video. To achieve this, the scene is assumed to be static (i.e., rigid), while the only motion is that of the camera. However, this causes degenerate behaviour in the depth estimator when this assumption is broken. To deal with this issue, the paper [388] includes a predictive masking which learns to ignore regions that violates the rigidity assumptions. Vijayanarasimhan *et al.* [339] propose a more complex motion model based on multiple motion masks, and GeoNet model [374] decompose depth and optical flow to account for object motion within the image sequence. Self-supervised monocular trained methods have been further improved by constraining predicted depths to be consistent with surface normals [373], using pre-computed instance-level segmentation masks [38] and increasing the resolu tion of the input images [273]. Godard *et al.* [103] further close the performance gap between monocular and stereo-trained self-supervision with Monodepth2 which uses multi-scale estimation and a per-pixel minimum re-projection loss that better handles occlusions. We extend Monodepth2 with our proposed ideas, namely self-attention and discrete disparity volume.

6.2.2 Self-attention

Self-attention has improved the performance of natural language processing (NLP) systems by allowing a better handling of long-range dependencies between words [335], when compared with recurrent neural networks (RNN) [299], long short term memory (LSTM) [132], and convolutional neural nets (CNN) [199]. This better performance can be explained by the fact that RNNs, LSTMs and CNNs can only process information in the local word neighbourhood, making these approaches insufficient for capturing long range dependencies in a sentence [335], which is essential in some tasks, like machine translation. Self-attention has been proposed in computer vision for improving Image Classification and Object Drection [20,269]. Self-attention has also improved the performance of computer vision tasks such as semantic segmentation [376] by addressing more effectively the problem of segmenting visual classes in non-contiguous regions of the image, when compared with convolutional layers [42,44,385], which can only process information in the local pixel neighbourhood. In fact, many of the recent improvements in semantic segmentation performance stem from improved contextual aggregation strategies (i.e., strategies that can process spatially non-contiguous image regions) such as the Pyramid Pooling Module (PPM) in PSPNet [385], and the Atrous Spatial Pyramid Pooling [42]. In both of these methods, multiple scales of information are aggregated to improve the contextual representation by the network. Yuan *et al.* [376] further improve on this area with OCNet, which adds to a ResNet-101 [123] backbone a self-attention module that learns to contextually represent groups of features with similar semantic similarity. Therefore, we hypothesise that such self-attention mechanisms can also improve depth prediction using monocular video because the correct context for the prediction of a pixel depth may be at a non-contiguous location that the standard convolutions cannot reach.

6.2.3   Discrete Disparity Volume

Kendall *et al.* [168] propose to learn stereo matching in a supervised manner by using a shared CNN encoder with a cost volume that is refined using 3D convolutions. Liu *et al.* [213] investigate this idea further by training a model using monocular video with ground truth depth and poses. This paper [213] relies on a depth probability volume (DPV) and a Bayesian filtering framework that refines outliers based on the uncertainty computed from the DPV. Fu *et al.* [88] represent their ground-truth depth data as discrete bins, effectively forming a disparity volume for training. All methods above work in fully-supervised scenarios, showing advantages for depth estimation robustness and sharpness allied with the possibility of estimating depth uncertainty. Such uncertainty estimation can be used by autonomous systems to improve decision making [166] or to refine depth estimation [88]. In this paper, we hypothesis that the extension of self-supervised monocular trained methods with a discrete disparity volume will provide the same advantages observed in fully-supervised models.

6.3   Methods

In the presentation of our proposed model for self-supervised monocular trained depth estimation, we focus on showing the importance of the main contributions of this paper, namely self-attention and discrete disparity volume. We use as baseline, the Monodepth2 model [103] based on a UNet architecture [294].

6.3.1   Model

We represent the RGB image with $\mathbf{I} : \Omega \to \mathbb{R}^3$, where Ω denotes the image lattice of height H and width W. The first stage of the model, depicted in Fig. 4.1, is the ResNet-101 encoder, which forms $\mathbf{X} = resnet_\theta(\mathbf{I}_t)$, with $\mathbf{X} : \Omega_{1/8} \to \mathbb{R}^M$, M denoting the number of channels at the output of the ResNet, and $\Omega_{1/8}$ representing the low-resolution lattice at $(1/8)^{th}$ of its initial size in Ω. The ResNet output is then used by the self-attention module [347], which first forms the query, key and value results, represented by:

$$f(\mathbf{X}(\omega)) = \mathbf{W}_f\mathbf{X}(\omega),$$
$$g(\mathbf{X}(\omega)) = \mathbf{W}_g\mathbf{X}(\omega), \tag{6.1}$$
$$h(\mathbf{X}(\omega)) = \mathbf{W}_h\mathbf{X}(\omega),$$

respectively, with $\mathbf{W}_f, \mathbf{W}_g, \mathbf{W}_h \in \mathbb{R}^{N \times M}$. The query and key values are then combined with

$$\mathbf{S}_\omega = softmax(f(\mathbf{X}(\omega))^T g(\mathbf{X})), \tag{6.2}$$

where $\mathbf{S}_\omega : \Omega_{1/8} \to [0,1]$, and we abuse the notation by representing $g(\mathbf{X})$ as a tensor of size $N \times H/8 \times W/8$. The self-attention map is then built by the multiplication of value and $\mathbf{S}_\omega$ in (6.2), with:

$$\mathbf{A}(\omega) = \sum_{\tilde{\omega} \in \Omega_{1/8}} h(\mathbf{X}(\tilde{\omega})) \times \mathbf{S}_\omega(\tilde{\omega}), \tag{6.3}$$

with $\mathbf{A} : \Omega_{1/8} \to \mathbb{R}^N$.

The low-resolution discrete disparity volume (DDV) is denoted by $\mathbf{D}_{1/8}(\omega) = conv_{3\times3}(\mathbf{A}(\omega))$, with $\mathbf{D}_{1/8} : \Omega_{1/8} \to \mathbb{R}^K$ (K denotes the number of discretized disparity values), and $conv_{3\times3}(.)$ denoting a convolutional layer with filters of size 3×3. The low resolution disparity map is then computed with

$$\sigma(\mathbf{D}_{1/8}(\omega)) = \sum_{k=1}^{K} softmax(\mathbf{D}_{1/8}(\omega)[k]) \times disparity(k), \tag{6.4}$$

where $softmax(\mathbf{D}_{1/8}(\omega)[k])$ is the softmax result of the kth output from $\mathbf{D}_{1/8}$, and $disparity(k)$ holds the disparity value for k. Given the ambiguous results produced by these low-resolution disparity maps, we follow the multi-scale strategy proposed by Godard *et al.* [103]. The low resolution map from (6.4) is the first step of the multi-scale decoder that consists of three additional stages of upconv operators (i.e., nearest upsample + convolution) that receive skip connections from the ResNet encoder for the respective resolutions, as shown in Fig. 4.1. These skip connections between encoding layers and associated decoding layers are known to retain high-level information in the final depth output. At each resolution, we form a new DDV, which is used to compute the disparity map at that particular resolution. The resolutions considered are $(1/8)$, $(1/4)$, $(1/2)$, and $(1/1)$ of the original resolution, respectively represented by $\sigma(\mathbf{D}_{1/8})$, $\sigma(\mathbf{D}_{1/4})$, $\sigma(\mathbf{D}_{1/2})$, and $\sigma(\mathbf{D}_{1/1})$.

Another essential part of our model is the pose estimator [388], which takes two images recorded at two different time steps, and returns the relative transformation as in

$$\mathbf{T}_{t \to t'} = p_\phi(\mathbf{I}_t, \mathbf{I}_{t'}), \tag{6.5}$$

where $\mathbf{T}_{t \to t'}$ denotes the transformation matrix between images recorded at time steps t and t', and $p_\phi(.)$ is the pose estimator, consisting of a deep learning model parameterised by ϕ.

6.3.2   Training and Inference

The training is based on the minimum per-pixel photometric re-projection error [103] between the source image $\mathbf{I}_{t'}$ and the target image $\mathbf{I}_t$, using the relative pose $\mathbf{T}_{t \to t'}$ defined in (6.5). The pixel-wise error is defined by

$$\ell_p = \frac{1}{|\mathcal{S}|} \sum_{s \in \mathcal{S}} \left(\min_{t'} \mu^{(s)} \times pe(\mathbf{I}_t, \mathbf{I}_{t \to t'}^{(s)}) \right), \tag{6.}$$

where $pe(.)$ denotes the photometric reconstruction error, $\mathcal{S} = \{\frac{1}{8}, \frac{1}{4}, \frac{1}{2}, \frac{1}{1}\}$ is the set of the resolutions available for the disparity map, defined in (6.4), $t' \in \{t-1, t+1\}$ indicating that we use two frames that are temporally adjacent to $\mathbf{I}_t$ as its source frames [103], and $\mu^{(s)}$ is a binary mask that filters out stationary points (see more details below in Eq.6.10) [103]. The re-projected image in (6.6) is defined by

$$\mathbf{I}_{t \to t'}^{(s)} = \mathbf{I}_{t'}\langle proj(\sigma(\mathbf{D}_t^{(s)}), \mathbf{T}_{t \to t'}, \mathbf{K}) \rangle, \tag{6}$$

where $proj(.)$ represents the 2D coordinates of the projected depths $\mathbf{D}_t$ in $\mathbf{I}_{t'}$, $\langle . \rangle$ the sampling operator, and $\sigma(\mathbf{D}_t^{(s)})$ is defined in (6.4). Similarly to [103], the pre-computed intrinsics $\mathbf{K}$ of all images are identical, and we use bi-linear sampling to sample the source images and

$$pe(\mathbf{I}_t, \mathbf{I}_{t'}^{(s)}) = \frac{\alpha}{2}(1 - \text{SSIM}(\mathbf{I}_t, \mathbf{I}_{t'}^{(s)})) + (1 - \alpha)\|\mathbf{I}_t - \mathbf{I}_{t'}^{(s)}\|_1, \tag{}$$

where $\alpha = 0.85$. Following [101] we use an edge-aware smoothness regularisation term to improve the predictions around object boundaries:

$$\ell_s \quad = \quad |\partial_x d_t^*| \, e^{-|\partial_x \mathbf{I}_t|} + |\partial_y d_t^*| \, e^{-|\partial_y \mathbf{I}_t|}, \tag{6.9}$$

where $d_t^* = d_t / \overline{d}_t$ is the mean-normalized inverse depth from [342] to discourage shrinking of the estimated depth. The auto-masking of stationary points [103] in (6.6) is necessary because the assumptions of a moving camera and a static scene are not always met in self-supervised monocular trained depth estimation methods [103]. This masking filters out pixels that remain with the same appearance between two frames in a sequence, and is achieved with a binary mask defined as

$$\mu^{(s)} = \left[\min_{t'} pe(\mathbf{I}_t, \mathbf{I}^{(s)}_{t' \to t}) < \min_{t'} pe(\mathbf{I}_t, \mathbf{I}_{t'}) \right], \tag{6.10}$$

where [.] represents the Iverson bracket. The binary mask μ in (6.10) masks the loss in (6.6) to only include the pixels where the re-projection error of $\mathbf{I}^{(s)}_{t' \to t}$ is lower than the error of the un-warped image $\mathbf{I}_{t'}$, indicating that the visual object is moving relative to the camera. The final loss is computed as the weighted sum of the per-pixel minimum reprojection loss in (6.6) and smoothness term in (6.9),

$$\ell = \ell_p + \lambda \ell_s \tag{6.11}$$

where λ is the weighting for the smoothness regularisation term. Both the pose model and depth model are trained jointly using this photometric reprojection error. Inference is achieved by taking a test image at the input of the model and producing the high-resolution disparity map $\sigma(\mathbf{D}_{1/1})$.

6.4 Experiments

We train and evaluate our method using the KITTI 2015 stereo data set [95]. We also evaluate our method on the Make3D data set [304] using our model trained on KITTI 2015. We use the split and evaluation of Eigen *et al.* [73], and following previous works [103, 388], we remove static frames before training and only evaluate depths up to a fixed range of 80m [73, 94, 101, 103]. As with [103], this results in 39,810 monocular training sequences, consisting of sequences of three frames, with 4,424 validation sequences. As our baseline model, we use Monodepth2 [103],

Figure 6.3: **Qualitative results on the KITTI Eigen split [73] test set.** Our models
perform better on thinner objects such as trees, signs and bollards, as well as being
better at delineating difficult object boundaries.

but we replace the original ResNet-18 by a ResNet-101 that has higher capacity, but requires more memory. To address this memory issue, we use the inplace activated batch normalisation [297], which fuses the batch normalization layer and the activation functions to reach up to 50% memory savings.

As self-supervised monocular trained depth estimators do not contain scale information, we use the per-image median ground truth scaling [103, 388].Following architecture best practices from the Semantic Segmentation community, we adopt the *atrous convolution* [43], also known as the *dilated convolution*, in the last two convolutional blocks of the ResNet-101 encoder [43,44,376,385] with dilation rates of 2 and 4, respectively. This has been shown to significantly improve multi-scale encoding by increasing the models field-of-view [43]. The results for the quantitative analysis are shown in Sec. 6.4.2. We also present an ablation study comparing the effects of the our different contributions in Sec. 6.4.4. Final models are selected using the lowest absolute relative error metric on the validation set.

6.4.1 Implementation Details

Our system is trained using the PyTorch library [270], with models trained on a single Nvidia 2080Ti for 20 epochs. We jointly optimize both our pose and depth networks with the Adam Optimizer [173] with $\beta_1 = 0.9$, $\beta_2 = 0.999$ and a learning rate of $1e^{-4}$. We use a single learning rate decay to $lr = 1e^{-5}$ after 15 epochs. As with previous papers [103], our ResNet encoders use pre-trained ImageNet [300] weights as this has been show to reduce training time and improve overall accuracy of the predicted depths. All models are trained using the following data augmentations with 50% probability; Horizontal flips, random contrast (±0.2), saturation (±0.2), hue jitter (±0.1) and brightness (±0.2). Crucially, augmentations are only performed on the images input into the depth and pose network and the loss in (6.11) is computed using the original ground truth images, with the smoothness term set to $\lambda = 1e^{-3}$. Image resolution is set to 640×192 pixels.

Method	Train	Abs Rel	Sq Rel	RMSE	RMSE log	$\delta < 1.25$	$\delta < 1.25^2$	$\delta < 1.25^3$
Eigen [74]	D	0.203	1.548	6.307	0.282	0.702	0.890	0.890
Liu [215]	D	0.201	1.584	6.471	0.273	0.680	0.898	0.967
Klodt [178]	D*M	0.166	1.490	5.998	-	0.778	0.919	0.966
AdaDepth [253]	D*	0.167	1.257	5.578	0.237	0.771	0.922	0.971
Kuznietsov [189]	DS	0.113	0.741	4.621	0.189	0.862	0.960	0.986
DVSO [371]	D*S	0.097	0.734	4.442	0.187	0.888	0.958	0.980
SVSM FT [227]	DS	0.094	0.626	4.252	0.177	0.891	0.965	0.984
Guo [113]	DS	0.096	0.641	4.095	0.168	0.892	0.967	0.986
DORN [88]	D	0.072	0.307	2.727	0.120	0.932	0.984	0.994
Zhou [388]†	M	0.183	1.595	6.709	0.270	0.734	0.902	0.959
Yang [373]	M	0.182	1.481	6.501	0.267	0.725	0.906	0.963
Mahjourian [229]	M	0.163	1.240	6.220	0.250	0.762	0.916	0.968
GeoNet [374]†	M	0.149	1.060	5.567	0.226	0.796	0.935	0.975
DDVO [342]	M	0.151	1.257	5.583	0.228	0.810	0.936	0.974
DF-Net [397]	M	0.150	1.124	5.507	0.223	0.806	0.933	0.973
LEGO [372]	M	0.162	1.352	6.276	0.252	-	-	-
Ranjan [284]	M	0.148	1.149	5.464	0.226	0.815	0.935	0.973
EPC++ [225]	M	0.141	1.029	5.350	0.216	0.816	0.941	0.976
Struct2depth '(M)' [38]	M	0.141	1.026	5.291	0.215	0.816	0.945	0.979
Monodepth2 [103]	M	0.115	0.903	4.863	0.193	0.877	0.959	0.981
Monodepth2 (1024 × 320) [103]	M	0.115	0.882	4.701	0.190	0.879	0.961	0.982
Ours	**M**	**0.106**	**0.861**	**4.699**	**0.185**	**0.889**	**0.962**	**0.982**
Garg [94]†	S	0.152	1.226	5.849	0.246	0.784	0.921	0.967
Monodepth R50 [101]†	S	0.133	1.142	5.533	0.230	0.830	0.936	0.970
StrAT [237]	S	0.128	1.019	5.403	0.227	0.827	0.935	0.971
3Net (R50) [276]	S	0.129	0.996	5.281	0.223	0.831	0.939	0.974
3Net (VGG) [276]	S	0.119	1.201	5.888	0.208	0.844	0.941	0.978
SuperDepth + pp [273] (1024 × 382)	S	0.112	0.875	4.958	0.207	0.852	0.947	0.977
Monodepth2 [103]	S	0.109	0.873	4.960	0.209	0.864	0.948	0.975
Monodepth2 (1024 × 320) [103]	S	0.107	0.849	4.764	0.201	0.874	0.953	0.977
UnDeepVO [206]	MS	0.183	1.730	6.57	0.268	-	-	-
Zhan FullNYU [379]	D*MS	0.135	1.132	5.585	0.229	0.820	0.933	0.971
EPC++ [225]	MS	0.128	0.935	5.011	0.209	0.831	0.945	0.979
Monodepth2 [103]	MS	0.106	0.818	4.750	0.196	0.874	0.957	0.979
Monodepth2(1024 × 320) [103]	MS	0.106	0.806	4.630	0.193	0.876	0.958	0.980

Table 6.1: **Quantitative results.** Comparison of existing methods to our own on the KITTI 2015 [95] using the Eigen split [73]. The Best results are presented in **bold** for each category, with second best results underlined. The supervision level for each method is presented in the *Train* column with; D – Depth Supervision D* – Auxiliary depth supervision, S – Self-supervised stereo supervision, M – Self supervised mono supervision. Results are presented without any post-processing [101], unless marked with – + pp. If newer results are available on github, these are marked with – †. Non-Standard resolutions are documented along with the method name. Metrics indicated by red: *lower is better*, Metrics indicated by blue *higher is better*

6.4.2 KITTI Results

The results for the experiment are presented in Table 6.1. When comparing ou method (grayed row in Table 6.1) on the KITTI 2015 data set [95] (using Eigen [73 split), we observe that we outperform all existing self-supervised monocular trained methods by a significant margin. Compared to other methods that rely on stronger supervision signals (e.g., stereo supervision and mono+stereo supervision), our approach is competitive, producing comparable results to the current state of the art method Monodepth2. As can be seen in Figure 5.3 our method shows sharper results on thinner structures such as poles than the baseline Monodepth2. In general, Monodepth2 (Mono and Mono+Stereo) struggles with thin structures that overlap with foliage, while our method is able to accurately estimate the depth of these smaller details. We attribute this to the combination of the dilated convolutions and the contextual information from the self-attention module. As can be seen in car windows, Monodepth2 and our method struggle to predict the depth on glassy reflective surfaces. However, this is a common issue observed in self-supervised methods because they cannot accurately predict depth for transparent surfaces since the photometric reprojection/warping error is ill-defined for such materials/surfaces. For instance, in the example of car windows, the correct depth that would minimise the photometric reprojection loss is actually the depth from the car interior, instead of the glass depth, as would be recorded by the ground truth LiDAR. When comparing our method against some specific error cases for Monodepth2 [103] (Figure 6.4), we can see that our method succeeds in estimating depth of the highly reflective car roof (*left*) and successfully disentangles the street sign from the background (*right*). This can be explained by the extra context and receptive field afforded by the self-attention context module as well as the regularisation provided by the discrete disparity volume.

6.4.3 Make3D Results

Table 6.2 presents the quantitative results for the Make3D data set [304] using our model trained on KITTI2015. We follow the same testing protocol as Monodepth2 [103] and methods are compared using the evaluation criteria outline in [101]. It can be seen in Table 6.2 that our method produces superior results compared with previous methods that also rely on self-supervision.

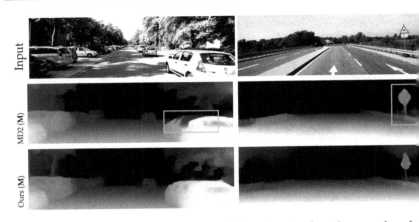

Figure 6.4: **Monodepth2 Failure cases.** Although trained on the same loss fu tion as the monocular trained (**M**) Monodepth2 [103], our method succeeds estimating depth for the reflective car roof *(Left)* and the difficult to delineate st sign *(Right)*.

	Type	Abs Rel	Sq Rel	RMSE	$\log_{10}$
Karsch [162]	D	0.428	5.079	8.389	0.149
Liu [216]	D	0.475	6.562	10.05	0.165
Laina [192]	D	**0.204**	**1.840**	**5.683**	**0.084**
Monodepth [101]	S	0.544	10.94	11.760	0.193
Zhou [388]	M	0.383	5.321	10.470	0.478
DDVO [342]	M	0.387	4.720	8.090	0.204
Monodepth2 [103]	M	0.322	3.589	7.417	0.163
Ours	M	**0.297**	**2.902**	**7.013**	**0.158**

Table 6.2: **Make3D results.** All self-supervised mono (M) models use med scaling.

6.4.4 Ablation Study

Table 6.3 shows an ablation study of our method, where we start from the base Monodepth2 [103] (row 1). Then, by first adding DDV (row 2) and both attention and DDV (row 3), we observe a steady improvement in almost

Backbone	Self-Attn	DDV	Abs Rel	Sq Rel	RMSE	RMSE log	$\delta < 1.25$	$\delta < 1.25^2$	$\delta < 1.25^3$
Baseline (MD2 ResNet18)	✗	✗	0.115	0.903	4.863	0.193	0.877	0.959	0.981
ResNet18	✗	✓	0.112	0.838	4.795	0.191	0.877	0.960	0.981
ResNet18	✓	✗	0.112	0.845	4.769	0.19	0.877	0.96	0.982
ResNet18	✓	✓	0.111	0.941	4.817	0.189	0.885	0.961	0.981
ResNet101 w/ Dilated Conv	✗	✗	0.110	0.876	4.853	0.189	0.879	0.961	0.982
ResNet101 w/ Dilated Conv	✗	✓	0.110	0.840	4.765	0.189	0.882	0.961	0.982
ResNet101 w/ Dilated Conv	✓	✗	0.108	0.808	4.754	0.185	0.885	0.962	0.982
ResNet101 w/ Dilated Conv	✓	✓	0.106	0.861	4.699	0.185	0.889	0.962	0.982

Table 6.3: **Ablation Study.** Results for different versions of our model with comparison to our baseline model Monodepth2 [103](MD2 ResNet18). We evaluate the impact of the Discrete Disparity Volume (DDV), Self-Attention Context module and the larger network architecture. All models were trained with Monocular self-supervision. Metrics indicated by red: *lower is better*, Metrics indicated by blue: *higher is better*

evaluation measures. We then switch the underlying encoding model ResNet-18 to ResNet-101 with dilated convolutions in row 4. Rows 5 and 6 show the addition of DDV and then both self-attention and DDV, respectively, again with a steady improvement of evaluation results in almost all evaluation measures. The DDV on the smaller ResNet-18 model provides a large improvement over the baseline in the *absolute relative* and *squared relative* measures. However, ResNet-101 shows only a small improvement over the baseline when using the DDV. The Self-Attention mechanism drastically improves the close range accuracy ($\delta < 1.25$) for both backbone models. The significantly larger improvement of the self-attention module in the ResNet-101 model (row 6), is likely because of the large receptive field produced by the dilated convolutions, which increases the amount of contextual information that can be computed by the self-attention operation.

6.4.5 Self-attention and Depth Uncertainty

While the self-attention module and DDV together provide significant quantitative and qualitative improvements, they also provide secondary functions. The attention maps (Eq. 6.3) from the self-attention module can be visualized to interrogate the relationships between objects and disparity learnt by the model. The attention maps highlight non-contiguous image regions (Fig. 6.5), focusing on either foreground, midground or background regions. The maps also tend to highlight either distant objects or stationary visual objects, like cars. Moreover, as the DDV encodes a probability over a disparity ray, using discretized bins, it is possible to compute the uncertainty for each ray by measuring the variance of the probability distribution. Figure 6.6 shows a trend where uncertainty increases with distance, up until the background image regions, which are estimated as near-infinite to infinite depth with very low uncertainty. This has also been observed in supervised models that are capable of estimating uncertainty [213]. Areas of high foliage and high shadow (row 2) show very high uncertainty, likely attributed to the low contrast and lack of textural detail in these regions.

Figure 6.5: **Attention maps from our network**. Subset of the attention maps produced by our method. Blue indicates region of attention.

Figure 6.6: **Uncertainty from our network**. The Discrete Disparity Volume allows us to compute pixel-wise depth uncertainty. Blue indicates areas of low uncertainty, green/red regions indicate areas of high/highest uncertainty.

6.5   Conclusions and Future Work

In this paper we have presented a method to address the challenge of learning to predict accurate disparities solely from monocular video. By incorporating a self-attention mechanism to improve the contextual information available to the model, we have achieved state of the art results for monocular trained self-supervised depth estimation on the KITTI 2015 [95] dataset and Make3D datasets [303]. Additionally, we regularised the training of the model by using a discrete disparity volume, which allows us to produce more robust and sharper depth estimates and to compute pixel-wise depth uncertainties. In the future, we plan to investigate the benefits of incorporating self-attention in the pose model as well as using the estimated uncertainties for outlier filtering and volumetric fusion.

Supplementary

6.6 KITTI Improved Ground Truth

The evaluation method that was introduced by Eigen *et al.* [73] uses reprojected LiDAR points to create the ground truth depth images. However, the reprojections do not handle occlusions, non-rigid motion or motion from the camera. Uhrig *et al.* [330] introduced an improved set of high quality ground truth depth maps for the KITTI dataset. These high quality images are instead reprojected using 5 consecutive LiDAR frames and uses the stereo images for better handling of occlusions. To obviate the need of retraining, as with other work [103], we use a modified Eigen [73] test split on the images that overlap between these datasets. This results in 652 (93%) of the 697 original test frames being retained. We use the same evaluation strategy and metrics as discussed in the Experiments section of the main paper. The results of this analysis can be found in Table 6.4.

6.7 Network Architecture

For all experiments, except where noted, we use a ResNet-101 encoder model with pretrained ImageNet weights. This model has been modified to use atrous/dilation convolutions [43] in the final two residual blocks. We use rectified linear activation (ReLU) in the encoding model and the Exponential Linear Unit (ELU) in the decoder. Skip connections are applied to the two intermediate outputs between the encoder and decoder. As the internal resolution is much larger than that of the ResNet-18 used by Monodepth2 [103] ($\frac{1}{8}$ scale compared with $\frac{1}{32}$ scale), a skip connection is not required for the smallest output resolution. For the pose model we use the same ResNet-18 and pose decoder defined by Monodepth2 [103]. The full depth network architecture can be found in Table 6.5.

Method	Train	Abs Rel	Sq Rel	RMSE	RMSE log	$\delta < 1.25$	$\delta < 1.25^2$	$\delta < 1.25^3$
Zhou [388]†	M	0.176	1.532	6.129	0.244	0.758	0.921	0.971
Mahjourian [229]	M	0.134	0.983	5.501	0.203	0.827	0.944	0.981
GeoNet [374]	M	0.132	0.994	5.240	0.193	0.833	0.953	0.985
DDVO [342]	M	0.126	0.866	4.932	0.185	0.851	0.958	0.986
Ranjan [284]	M	0.123	0.881	4.834	0.181	0.860	0.959	0.985
EPC++ [225]	M	0.120	0.789	4.755	0.177	0.856	0.961	0.987
Monodepth2 [103] w/o pretraining	M	0.112	0.715	4.502	0.167	0.876	0.967	0.990
Monodepth2 [103]	M	0.090	0.545	3.942	0.137	0.914	0.983	0.995
Ours	M	**0.081**	**0.484**	**3.716**	**0.126**	**0.927**	**0.985**	**0.996**
Monodepth [101]	S	0.109	0.811	4.568	0.166	0.877	0.967	0.988
3net [276] (VGG)	S	0.119	0.920	4.824	0.182	0.856	0.957	0.985
3net [276] (ResNet 50)	S	0.102	0.675	4.293	0.159	0.881	0.969	0.991
SuperDepth [273] + pp	S	0.090	0.542	3.967	0.144	0.901	0.976	**0.993**
Monodepth2 [103] w/o pretraining	S	0.110	0.849	4.580	0.173	0.875	0.962	0.986
Monodepth2 [103]	S	**0.085**	**0.537**	**3.868**	**0.139**	**0.912**	**0.979**	**0.993**
Zhan FullNYU [379]	D*MS	0.130	1.520	5.184	0.205	0.859	0.955	0.981
EPC++ [225]	MS	0.123	0.754	4.453	0.172	0.863	0.964	0.989
Monodepth2 [103] w/o pretraining	MS	0.107	0.720	4.345	0.161	0.890	0.971	0.989
Monodepth2 [103]	MS	**0.080**	**0.466**	**3.681**	**0.127**	**0.926**	**0.985**	**0.995**

Table 6.4: **Quantitative results on KITTI improved ground truth.** Comparison of existing methods to our own on the KITTI 2015 [95] using the improved ground truth [330] of the Eigen test split [73]. The Best results are presented in **bold** for each category, with second best results underlined. The supervision level for each method is presented in the *Train* column with; D – Depth Supervision, D* – Auxiliary depth supervision, S – Self-supervised stereo supervision, M – Self-supervised mono supervision. Results are presented without any post-processing [101], unless marked with – + pp. If newer results are available on github, these are marked with – †. Non-Standard resolutions are documented along with the method name. Metrics indicated by red: *lower is better*, Metrics indicated by blue: *higher is better*

Depth Network							
layer	k	s	ch	dilation	res	input	activation
conv1	3	1	64	2	1	image	ReLU
conv2	3	1	64	1	2	conv1	ReLU
conv3	3	1	128	1	2	conv2	ReLU
maxpool	3	2	128	1	2	conv2	ReLU
res1	3	1	256	1	4	conv3	ReLU
res2	3	2	512	1	8	res1	ReLU
res3	3	1	1024	2	8	res2	ReLU
res4	3	1	2048	4	8	res4	ReLU
context	3	1	512	1	8	res4	Self-Attn
ddv4	3	1	128	1	8	context	Linear
disp4	3	1	1	1	8	ddv1	softmax
upconv3	3	1	64	1	8	ddv4	ELU
deconv3	3	1	64	1	4	upconv3↑, res1	ELU
ddv3	3	1	128	1	4	deconv3	Linear
disp3	3	1	1	1	4	ddv3	softmax
upconv2	3	1	64	1	4	deconv3	ELU
deconv2	3	1	64	1	2	upconv2↑, conv3	ELU
ddv2	3	1	128	1	2	deconv2	Linear
disp2	3	1	1	1	2	ddv2	softmax
upconv1	3	1	32	1	2	deconv2	ELU
deconv1	3	1	32	1	1	upconv1↑	ELU
ddv1	3	1	128	1	1	deconv1	Linear
disp1	3	1	1	1	1	ddv1	softmax

Table 6.5: **Network architecture.** This table details the kernel size (**k**), str (**s**), output channels (**ch**) dilation factor (**dilation**), resolution scale (**res**), in features for each layer (**input**) and activation function (**activation**) used in model. Layers marked with ↑ represent a 2× nearest-neighbour upsampling be passing to the convolutional layer. Residual blocks are denoted by *res*∗ nam convention. Each convolution and residual block also uses batch normalisat in the form of a inplace activated batch normalisation [297]. The self-atten module (*context*) is denoted as having an activation of *Self-Attn*.

6.7.1 Additional Qualitative Results

In Figure 6.7, we present additional qualitative comparisons to multiple previous works. Our method produces sharper predictions for thin structures and complex shapes such as people. In Figure 6.8, we show the uncertainty estimates for multiple images. As can been seen in the figure, areas of low contrast (row 2) correspond with areas of high uncertainty. Moreover, high uncertainty can also be observed in areas of unknown texture (row 7, right hand side). This area of the input image also demonstrates issues with texture copy artefacts [103] in the predicted depth. Additional attention maps are displayed in Figure 6.9. The attention maps were selected at random from the 512 output channels in the context module.

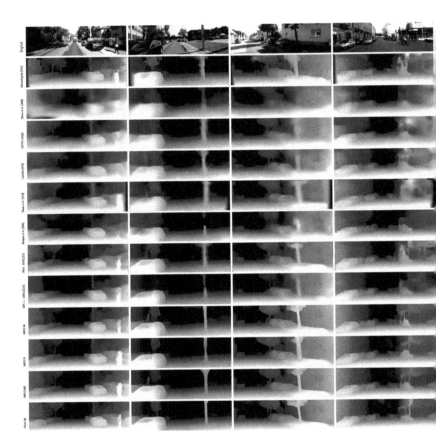

Figure 6.7: **Additional Qualitative Comparison.** A comparison of our method (*last row*) with several other methods for monocular and stereo trained self supervised depth estimation.

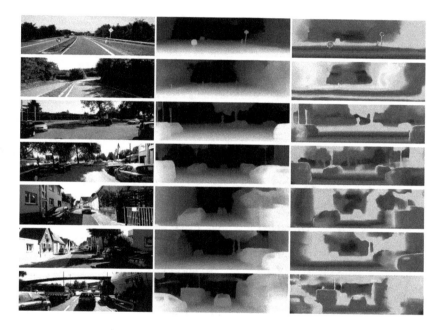

Figure 6.8: **Additional uncertainty results** The Discrete Disparity Volume (DDV) allows us to compute pixel-wise depth uncertainty by measuring the variance across the disparity *ray*. Left: Input Image, Middle: Depth prediction, Right: Uncertainty (Blue indicates areas of low uncertainty, green/red regions indicate areas of high/highest uncertainty).

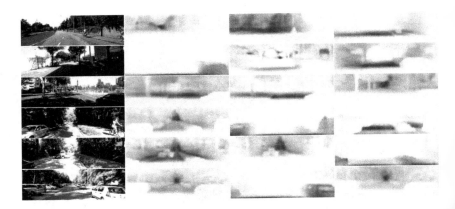

Figure 6.9: **Additional attention maps** selected at random from the output of context module (Blue indicates areas of high attention).

CHAPTER 7

Further Discussion and Conclusions

3D reconstruction has long been one of the key tasks in the field of Computer Vision, with many scientific and industry applications. In recent years, deep learning has been applied to this fundamental problem in an attempt to resolve many issues that exist with traditional reconstruction methods. However, using deep learning techniques for 3D reconstruction poses many of its own challenges. In this thesis, we have investigated multiple techniques to address the challenges of computation inefficiency and data scarcity when training deep neural networks for single view monocular 3D reconstruction. Initial methods for 3D reconstruction using deep learning relied heavily on the use of 3D volumes for representing object surfaces. These representations were selected due to the simplicity of integration with convolutional neural networks. However, when compared with standard image based Convolutional Neural Networks, volumetric representations require significantly more memory and computational resources.

In Chapter 4, we introduced a method for efficiently reconstructing high resolution 3D volumes by forcing the neural network to learn a compressed frequency domain representation using a novel Inverse Discrete Cosine Transform layer. By replacing the convolutional decoder of the network with our IDCT layer, we showed that it is possible to simultaneously increase volumetric resolution, reduce computation cost, and reduce the use of GPU memory, all by an order of magnitude without any loss of reconstruction quality.

While our IDCT layer results in efficient and accurate reconstructions, there a
some limitations to this method. Firstly, as the network uses a fully connec
layer to output the DCT coefficients, the number of parameters in the model c
increase exponentially with the number of DCT coefficients. Secondly, the num
of coefficients, and therefore the compression ratio, has to be selected ahead
time resulting in a model that can only reconstruct at fixed rates. Finally, as
IDCT decompression is a lossy process, there can be distinctive artefacts in
final reconstructed volumes, resulting in sub-optimal reconstruction quality. T
work could be further improved by changing the reconstruction to use "loc
patches or blocks, rather than a globally compressed volume. Similarly to ima
compression techniques that utilise DCT (e.g., JPEG), smaller fixed size regic
of the volume could be represented independently. This would allow the mo
to further exploit the sparsity of the 3D binary volumes, thereby reducing
number of parameters required and improving the compression of the volum

Contemporary work by Riegler *et al.* [292] proposed to improve the computatio
efficiency of volumetric CNNs by using multiple specialised network layers ba
on an Octree data structure. However, this work was limited in applicability to
binary volumes and point clouds. Alternatively, more recent methods [51,108,2
have generalised this approach to work for N-dimensional data by using Spa
Convolutional and Pooling layers. While 3D volumes represent a conveni
representation, due to the inefficiencies mentioned above, many researchers h
instead moved to using other representations such as Point Clouds [78,143,211
Meshes [111].

Another key concern of using Deep Learning for 3D reconstruction is the l
ited amount of data available for training. While image, text and audio datas
have grown in scale and availability, datasets of 3D models for both objects a
scenes, are limited in quality and size. This is attributed to the difficulties in cap
ing or modelling 3D surfaces, often requiring many man hours to acquire a sir
instance. In Chapter 5, we address the issue of data availability by leveraging
advances in generative modelling and self-supervision. We achieve this by l
training a model that predicts a set of fixed novel viewpoints for an object, gi

a single input image. Reconstructing novel view points naively, typically results in blurry images as non-visible regions of the object could have many plausible reconstructions. To remedy this, we also applied adversarial and feature matching losses to improve reconstruction quality. Simultaneously, we trained a depth estimator that utilises self-supervision, in the form of a photometric re-projection loss, on pairs of images of the same objects. The two models can be combined at inference time to reconstruct 3D point clouds, by first predicting a set of novel points for a test image, then predicting depth using the depth estimator for each of the novel view images. Finally, the synthesised RGB and depth images can be un-projected into a textured point cloud, using the known intrinsic and extrinsic camera matrices for the original dataset. We showed that by combining a Deep Generative Adversarial Network trained to perform novel view prediction and a monocular self-supervised depth estimator, it was possible to perform 3D point cloud reconstruction without any ground truth 3D data.

In practice, we found that training the Generative Adversarial Network for Novel View prediction was challenging because the model would mode collapse and produce novel views that could not be used for point cloud synthesis. We hypothesise that this is caused by the synthetically rendered images that were used for the training dataset as these images are not particularly realistic and have no background details. We believe that the adversarial training would have been more effective on a more realistic dataset. Another downside of this method is that it relies on having a dataset of fixed known points for every instance. In practice this would require using a camera rig with a set of fixed cameras to capture a real dataset. Our method could be further improved by having the model learn to predict novel viewpoints for any given camera pose.

Transformation-Grounded Image Generation Network for Novel 3D View Synthesis (TVSN) [267] was, at the time of its publication, the state of the art method for novel view prediction. While we did not reach state of the art results for novel view prediction, our method is not strictly comparable with TVSN. The TVSN method relies on direct supervision of an occlusion mask, optical flow and camera pose, for combining predicted pixels with observed pixels. Comparatively, our method does not require any supervision, and our novel view prediction results could be improved by including these extra supervisory signals to the network. Moreover, TVSN requires two networks to achieve the presented results, the first pass coarsely estimates the novel view point, while the second pass refines the prediction to improve textural details. In the future, we plan to extend our method to also use a second refinement network to further improve our results. Nevertheless, comparing with the unsupervised baseline results of TVSN, our method performs on par with the implementation presented by the authors [267], both qualitatively and quantitatively.

More recently, methods, such as *SynSin* [357], utilise differentiable rendering techniques to achieve impressive results on scene level novel view synthesis tasks. Differentiable rendering is a framework for incorporating 3D rendering methods, such as rasterization, into the deep learning framework. While most rendering techniques are differentiable and easily adapted, some are not and must be modified to be back-propagated through [46, 164, 218]. By incorporating differentiable rendering techniques into our method it would be possible to train the depth and novel view networks end-to-end, allowing us to further improve the results presented in Chapter 5.

Learning to reconstruct scenes, rather than objects, is a challenging task. Furthermore, capturing accurate 3D surfaces for scene level geometry is significantly more complicated than acquiring object level surfaces, mainly due to the many occlusions created by the complexity of the scene. Scene reconstruction focuses only on recovering the 3D surface information for visible pixels and traditionally this was achieved via stereo vision. Recently, there has been renewed interest in learning to predict depth from single view monocular images [73, 74, 94], due to the wide range of applications. Typically, these models are trained using ground truth depth information as supervision. In practice however, access to large and diverse RGB-D datasets is limited. Therefore, self-supervision has emerged as one possible method to train models without ground truth labels.

In Chapter 6, we improve upon the state of the art for self-supervised monocula depth estimation, evaluating our method on the KITTI 2015 [95] and Make3d [304] datasets. In that work, we hypothesise that by improving the receptive field of the estimator network, we could significantly improve the depth predictions. To achieve this, we incorporate a 2D self-attention module [347, 380], which allows the model to process information in a non-local neighbourhood, when compared with a standard 2D convolution. Furthermore, we change the model architecture of the baseline Monodepth2 [102] to use a larger architecture (ResNet-101) which includes dilated convolutions [43]. We further improve our method by utilising a probabilistic depth representation, which we call a Discrete Disparity Volume (DDV). The DDV is created by discretising the possible disparities between a minimum and maximum depth into a fixed number of "bins". We can then take a softmax across each disparity "ray", resulting in a probability for bin being the correct depth. Finally, the volume is projected into a disparity value by applying a *softargmax* operation. One major benefit of utilising the DDV, is that it allows us to compute the uncertainty of our depth predictions by measuring the variance of the distribution across the disparity bins.

The larger architecture and the self-attention module result in the model having significantly more parameters than the baseline method based on a ResNet-18 encoder and standard deconvolutional decoder. While on large powerful machines this does not necessarily pose much of a problem, one major use case of monocular depth estimators is in low-power embedded systems such as small drones, which may lack the computational performance and power budget for a binocular or active range-finding solution. One potential solution to this problem, would be to apply knowledge distillation [128] between the DDV's output by our method and a smaller more compact version with a smaller backbone model. Knowledge distillation is a technique for using a larger "teacher" model to supervise the training of a smaller "student" model. In many applications knowledge distillation has been shown to train student models that are more accurate than if that same model was trained without distillation [128]. By distilling a smaller network architecture with the knowledge of the significantly larger network architecture we used, it may be possible to reduce the compute and memory requirements without any significant drop in quantitative performance. This would allow our method to be run in environments with compute or memory constraints.

In Computer Vision tasks, it is common to apply the 2D self-attention globally over the representation produced by the backbone/encoder. Put simply, there is a single attention module which aggregates the non-local contextual information into a final feature representation which can be used for the downstream task, such as detection, segmentation, depth estimation, etc. This is the method of self-attention that we presented in Chapter 6. Recently, Bello *et al.* [20] and Ramachandran *et al.* [269] showed that by modifying all of the existing standard convolutional blocks used in the ResNet architecture to include 2D self-attention, it is possible to boost performance in image classification and object detection. Moreover, these authors [20, 269] show that adding positional encoding information to the convolutions used in the self-attention, leads to a significant increase in classification accuracy. By incorporating an architecture that utilises self-attention throughout the entire network, as well as positional encoding, we believe that the quality of the predictions from monocular depth estimators can be improved.

When performing self-supervised monocular depth estimation, it is required that a second network is used to estimate relative pose between consecutive frames. In our work, we did not modify the baseline pose model and left this as a ResNet 18 network. We believe that the joint pose estimation task could also benefit from the extra contextual information provided by the self-attention module and future work investigate network architectures for pose estimation that include self-attention.

While the work presented in this thesis focuses on volumetric and point cloud surface representations, newer implicit shape representations are being explored using Deep Learning. Deep Signed Distance Fields (DeepSDF) [268] and Neural Radiance Fields (NeRF) [243] represent objects and scenes respectively, by encoding 3D surfaces as continuous volumetric fields within the weights of a deep neural network. This allows for reconstructing higher quality 3D surfaces compared with standard volumetric representations, at the cost of an expensive sampling process during inference. Although the authors do not evaluate these method on single view reconstruction, implicitly encoding 3D shapes may result in higher quality reconstructions than those presented in this thesis (Chapter 4 and Chapter 5).

In this thesis, we have discussed several of the issues with using deep learning for single view 3D reconstruction. Our work utilises a novel Inverse Discrete Cosine Transform layer to address the computational inefficiencies with volumetric reconstruction. Using the IDCT layer we showed an order of magnitude improvement in volumetric resolution, memory consumption, training time and inference speed. By combining the recent advances in novel view prediction and depth estimation we have also addressed the issues surrounding the limited availability of training data for 3D reconstruction. We leveraged deep generative modelling and self-supervision to train a single-view 3D reconstruction system that requires only a small set of input images and no ground truth 3D training data.

We also improve self-supervised monocular depth estimation using 2D self-attention and a discrete disparity volume. This work resulted in a significant improvement to the monocular trained models, with state of the art quantitative results on the KITTI 2015 [95] and Make3d [304] datasets. Additionally, the 2D self-attention mechanism allow us to visualise saliency for each of the feature maps before they are transformed into disparities, potentially opening up avenues for understanding and interpreting the depth predictions from monocular depth estimators. Furthermore, for autonomous systems to make intelligent decisions, it is important for the system to understand which predictions are useful and trustworthy. To this end, the DDV can be used to measure uncertainty for each depth estimation. This is critically important, as certain features, such as texture-less regions or reflective surfaces, can result in noisy estimates and therefore potentially erroneous decisions.

The novel methods presented in this thesis will enable real-time procedural generation of 3D content for applications in Video Games, Virtual Reality and Augmented Reality, and improve 3D perception in many autonomous and robotic systems. In future, differentiable rendering and learnt 3D shape representations such as

NeRF [243], will lead to significant improvements in 3D reconstruction, enabling many exciting new applications in a variety of scientific and entertainment industries.

CPSIA information can be obtained
at www.ICGtesting.com
Printed in the USA
LVHW051309210623
750341LV00004B/254

Lyrics

Follow, follow the sun
And which way the wind blows
When this day is done
Breathe, breathe in the air
Set your intentions
Dream with care
Tomorrow's a new day for everyone
A brand new moon and brand new sun
So follow, follow the sun
The direction of the birds
The direction of love
Breathe, breathe in the air
Cherish this moment
Cherish this breath
Tomorrow's a new day for everyone
A brand new moon, brand new sun
When you feel life coming down on you like a heavyweight
When you feel this crazy society adding to the strain
Take a stroll to the nearest water's edge, remember your place
Many moons have risen and fallen long, long before you came
So which way is the wind blowing?
What does your heart say?
So follow, follow the sun
And which way the wind blows
When this day is done
Xavier Rudd

Bibliography

..., Destructful Angels—Blackness Rose. "Destructful Angels— BlacknessRose ..." Poemhunter.com. Accessed January 13, 2016. http://www.poemhunter.com/best-poems/blacknessrose/ destructful-angels/.

"Identify Snakes: A How-to Guide." Alderleaf Wilderness College. Accessed November 28, 2015. http://www.wildernesscollege.com/ identify-snakes.html.

"Amish Children." Amish Children. Accessed April 03, 2016. http:// www.welcome-to-lancaster-county.com/amish-children.html.

"The Definition of Twitterpated." Dictionary.com. Accessed March 15, 2016. http://www.dictionary.com/browse/twitterpated.

"Earthquakes in Hawai`i." Earthquakes in Hawai`i. Accessed December 5, 2015. http://hvo.wr.usgs.gov/earthquakes/.

"Elton John Lyrics: Sorry Seems To Be The Hardest Word." Elton John Lyrics: Sorry Seems To Be The Hardest Word. Accessed October 19, 2015. http://www.eltonography.com/songs/sorry_seems_to_be_ the_hardest_word.html.

"Multi-Dimensional." Multi-Dimensional. Accessed April 04, 2016. http:// www.evenstarcreations.com/index.php/multi-dimensional-70802.

"King James Bible." OFFICIAL KING JAMES BIBLE ONLINE: AUTHORIZED KING JAMES VERSION (KJV). Accessed April 26, 2016. http://www.kingjamesbibleonline.org/.

"The Vagus Nerve | Depression? Anxiety? Super (Self) Stimulating Subject Matter." Panic Attack Symptoms. Accessed February 09, 2016. http://chipur.com/the-vagus-nerve-depression-anxiety-super-self-stimulating-subject-matter.

"Quantum Energetics Foundation." Quantum Energetics Foundation. Accessed

December 31, 2015. http://quantumenergetics.org/quantumbiofeedback. html.

"Dragonfly Damselfly Power Animal Symbol Of Change Piercing Illusions Light Understanding Dreams." Shamanic Journey. Accessed March 27, 2016. http://www.shamanicjourney.com/dragonfly.

"Can Pyloric Stenosis Surgery Be Avoided?" Stories from the Survivors of Early Surgery. 2011. Accessed March 17, 2016. https:// survivinginfantsurgery.wordpress.com/2011/08/20/can-pyloric-stenosis-surgery-be avoided.

"How Rain Catchment Systems Works." The Water Project. Accessed December 5, 2015. http://thewaterproject.org/rain_catchment.

"Child Bible Songs." This Little Light of Mine. Accessed October 11, 2015. http://childbiblesongs.com/song-01-this-little-light-of-mine. shtml.

"Ostriches Don't Hide Their Heads in the Sand." Today I Found Out. August 12, 2010. Accessed August 8, 2015.http://www. todayifoundout.com/index.php/2010/08/ostriches-/dont-hide-their-heads-in-the-sand/.

Wikipedia. Accessed January 14, 2016. https://en.wikipedia.org/wiki/ Cerebral_hemorrhage.

Zimmermann, By. "Indian Culture: Traditions and Customs of India." LiveScience. January 30, 2015. Accessed October 10, 2015. http:// www.livescience.com/28634-indian-culture.html.

Chicago/Turabian formatting by BibMe.org.